The Great Career Paradox

When pursuing career success may not lead to career happines

Adrian Choo and Sze-Yen Chee

Foreword by Dr Vince Molinaro,
Author of New York Times Bestseller,
The Leadership Contract

BUSINESS
An imprint of Penguin Random House

PENGUIN BUSINESS

USA I Canada I UK I Ireland I Australia
New Zealand I India I South Africa I China I Southeast Asia

Penguin Business is part of the Penguin Random House group of companies
whose addresses can be found at global.penguinrandomhouse.com

Published by Penguin Random House SEA Pvt. Ltd
9, Changi South Street 3, Level 08-01,
Singapore 486361

First published in Penguin Business by Penguin Random House SEA 2022
Copyright © Adrian Choo and Sze-Yen Chee 2022

ISBN 9789814954723

Typeset in Adobe Caslon Pro by MAP Systems, Bengaluru, India

www.penguin.sg

Contents

Foreword

The world of work and careers has always been a passion for me. It started early in my career when I worked in a large public sector organization. We helped marginalized individuals in society get their lives back on track. We provided financial assistance, access to education programs, career development, and job search strategies.

I learned about the power of meaningful work in helping someone transform their lives for the better. When work has meaning, we feel we are making a difference and our lives are better—we are better employees, better spouses, better parents, and better friends.

As a career counsellor, it was my job to support my clients, bring them information about the changing world of work, and help them gain insights into their values, strengths, and interests.

A few years later, I realized that I had to change my own career. I discovered an entrepreneurial streak in me, so I left my government job to start my own career advisory company. My clients, primarily middle managers, brought me into their organizations to work with their teams.

This became my introduction to the field of leadership development, which has been my focus ever since. As a New York Times bestselling author, speaker, global executive and founder of Leadership Contract Inc, my team and I have the privilege of working with companies in twenty-five countries.

However, the career counsellor in me still exists. My passion for the world of work is still strong and what's clear to me is that effectively learning how to manage one's career is more critical now than ever before.

The global pandemic has upended the world of work. The workplace has become hybrid. Careers and meaningful jobs are no longer bound by geography or offices. The great resignation that we have seen is about people recognizing that they want more fulfilling careers and quality of life. Despite all these changes, I believe that there are many more opportunities for people to find fulfilling, meaningful work and create vibrant careers and lives.

But none of that will happen by accident. We will need new insights to help us navigate our careers in this new world of work.

Therefore, I'm so excited about this book, *The Great Career Paradox*, by Adrian Choo and Sze-Yen Chee, co-founders of Career Agility International—a sought-after and well-respected career advisory firm in Asia.

I have known and worked with Adrian for several years. Therefore, I can speak first-hand about his passion for helping his clients find meaningful career success. The book begins with a fundamental problem that Adrian and Yen observed in their work—so many professionals who seemed to achieve business and career success were unhappy. This problem was the inspiration for their book. On every page, you will find provocative ideas and practical insights to help you navigate your career in today's ever-changing world of work.

The book is bursting with key insights rooted in the authors' experiences in helping a cross-section of people—from CEOs and middle-managers to frontline employees—find personal purpose and happiness in their work.

If this sounds like you, then I would encourage you to pick up this book and use it as your how-to manual to guide your career during these times of change.

Good luck!

Dr Vince Molinaro
Founder and CEO
Leadership Contract Inc
New York Times Bestselling Author of *The Leadership Contract*

Why This Book Was Written

We came across a rather perplexing phenomenon many years ago when we were coaching a group of senior executives. The two of us were speaking to a client who was the CEO of a multi-million-dollar technology company. At the age of forty-three, he was, by any standard, a beacon of success in his industry. He was well respected by his peers, admired by many outside of his industry, and people scrambled to have him as their mentor. He was one of the highest paid executives in the industry. His list of achievements in the technology industry was as impressive as his charismatic ability to sway every senior business leader and investor in the room. In the eyes of many, he had reached the pinnacle of career success.

But one evening, over drinks, he shared with us a very dark secret. He said that despite his successful career, he was extremely unhappy.

'I stay awake at night anxious about next quarter's performance. I wonder how I will be judged and I worry whether my position as CEO will be taken over by a more ambitious, more capable person in my team. I am concerned about what people will think of me if I am unable to hold my position.'

He then leaned forward and showed me a bottle of pills he had removed from his jacket pocket.

It was a colourful mix of Prozac, Lexapro, Xanax—medicines prescribed by his physician to keep him calm under pressure.

'I can't sleep without these, and I can't perform without these either.'

'As Career Strategists, can you tell us what's wrong?'

We walked away from that meeting shaken that someone who had achieved so much success in his career could be so unhappy.

We wondered how many more 'successful' people out there were secretly unhappy with their careers and their lives, and why.

This encounter started us on a quest to find answers to what we term 'The Great Career Paradox'.

Why are people with seemingly successful careers unhappy?

In fact, from our observations, the further up the ladder they climb, the unhappier they become. These high-fliers complain about fatigue, lack of passion, and some even experience serious health problems. These cases are not isolated and have been documented many times before.

In August 2020, Matthew Cooper, CEO of EarnUp, a Silicon Valley Fintech managing more than $10 billion in loans was hospitalized for anxiety and depression and had to step down.[1]

Thankfully, he has since recovered and is a staunch advocate of Mental Wellness today.

As we delved deeper into this career paradox by studying and interviewing hundreds of business leaders, we uncovered one major reason behind why this was happening.

In their quest to thrive in the workplace or perhaps even just to survive in the corporate jungle, many executives have been single-mindedly pursuing 'success' without really pausing and thinking what that word really means to them.

---

[1] Scipioni, Jade, 'I want to help other people that are in pain': Inside a CEO's battle with mental health', *Make It*, May 6, 2021, https://www.cnbc.com/2021/05/06/inside-former-earnup-ceos-struggles-with-mental-health.html.

They have been taught from a very young age that success meant having lots of money, fancy job titles, owning that expensive car, or living in that exclusive part of town.

So, they focus all their efforts at work into achieving this, sacrificing all else at this altar of 'success'.

Unknowingly, they neglect their health, family, peace of mind, and even themselves in the pursuit of this ultimate goal.

Even when this 'success' had been achieved, they would still feel a deep sense of emptiness and personal unhappiness.

If left unaddressed, this sense of unfulfillment may lead the executive to drive even harder to achieve more at work, put in longer hours, and spend even less time on what could have made them truly happy, all in an effort to attain the elusive dream that is 'success'.

Hence the career paradox exists.

That is why some people, despite being at the highest echelons of corporate life and being the envy of many, secretly lead unhappy lives and inevitably, will either burn out, fall ill, or make frustrated decisions they might come to regret.

So, how do we avoid this career paradox?

We begin by realizing that in our haste to be successful, we might be chasing after the success that is valued by society but not by ourselves. Are we hankering after things that make us look good rather than things that would make us truly happy? Things like pursuing wealth instead of mental wellness or a good night's sleep? Or jostling for that prestigious corner office instead of spending time with family?

To be truly happy, we need to realign our thinking and begin with the end in mind.

Our ultimate goal should be achieving meaningful career success instead of just *any* measure of success. Meaningful career success is the collection of factors that truly matters to us and makes us happy. For some, this could be work-life balance, and for others, it could be work that changes the lives of others. Some might even see attaining professional development as meaningful career success.

We should identify what meaningful career success is to us and channel all our skills, energy, and effort into achieving them. Only then will you break out of the career paradox and start to enjoy true career happiness that will change your life for the better.

We have written this book to show you how, by focusing on meaningful career success, and through the use of various career strategies and by being skilled at Career Agility, you, too, can achieve personal happiness and live the life you deserve!

Happy reading!

Part A

Introduction

1

We're Not in Kansas Anymore, Toto

The Covid-19 pandemic changed the world forever. Economies were reinvented, industries were up-ended, and business models were disrupted. Indeed, the world of work had been irrevocably transformed.

Changing consumer trends and demand for new technologies meant that businesses had to transform and evolve to keep up, and their employees had to adapt even more quickly. Those that were unable to keep up had to restructure, downsize or shut down.

The resulting numbers of displaced workers troubled us greatly as many of them were unable to land jobs quickly, whilst those who managed to do so in record time intrigued us just as much.

And among those who managed to keep their jobs, a great degree of dissatisfaction was also recorded[2], leading to the great resignation of 2022—a mass exodus of workers from the corporate world.

There were seismic shifts in employment trends that resulted in anomalous situations like in the US where high unemployment

---

[2] Robinson, Bryan, 'Future Of Work: 8 Steps To Stop Employee Departures In 2022', *Forbes*, Dec 21, 2021, https://www.forbes.com/sites/bryanrobinson/2021/12/21/future-of-work-8-steps-to-stop-employee-departures-in-2022/?sh=135944ec513c.

numbers were ironically matched by the immense difficulty faced by companies trying to find talents to fill their job vacancies.[3]

Like Dorothy said to Toto in the 1939 movie, *The Wizard of Oz*, 'I've a feeling we're not in Kansas anymore,' the employment landscape is almost unrecognizable and the rules seem to have been rewritten in this post-pandemic world.

And yet, many of the executives we encounter are still holding on to their pre-2020 viewpoints, oblivious to the changes around them, or even paralysed by the fear of the unknown, hoping that things will revert to the 'good old days'.

This outdated thinking has little relevance to the 'new normal' and will endanger the employability and careers of those still clinging on to them.

That is why there is an urgency to write this book to update today's executives with the latest career thought leadership gathered from extensive research and interviews with hundreds of business leaders. It is our hope that by reading this book, you will gain an understanding of how important it is to change your thinking about careers, learn how to make adjustments, and thrive in your job for as long as you wish to continue working.

---

[3] Long, Heather, Fowers, Alyssa, Van Dam, Andrew, 'Why America has 8.4 million unemployed when there are 10 million job openings', *The Washington Post*, Sep 4, 2021, https://www.washingtonpost.com/business/2021/09/04/ten-million-job-openings-labor-shortage/.

Part B

Why We Need a New Model

2

An Unfamiliar Future Ahead

Life used to be a lot simpler in the past. You would study hard, get a good degree, join a large company or government organization, work hard, and stay in the role until you retired at 55 years old. However, things started to change somewhere in the 90s. People started living longer and healthier, and, suddenly, 55 became too early an age to exit the employment market.

Increasing cost of living and mounting housing debts also made the idea of not having an income after 55 rather unrealistic. In Singapore, the government's guideline on retirement age has been creeping upwards steadily—from 60 to 62, and now to 67—as a regulatory guideline for employers to continue hiring older workers.

With that much runway ahead of us and with disruptions due to technology and the pandemic, we all face a rather unfamiliar and uncomfortable future ahead.

Will I still have a job in 5 years' time? How do I remain employed? How can I compete against the younger and more agile graduates coming into the workforce?

How did the 'Rules of Employment' transform from 'Work hard in a 9–5 job until retirement' to 'Keep your head down and hope not to get retrenched' within one generation?

Let us share some of the ways careers have changed from being the old-school 'Version 1.0' to the disruptive 'Version 3.0' today. This is important because you will need to know these changes in order to thrive in the new environment that we are in now.

The Threat of Permanent Unemployability

True Career Stories: John, 48, Taxi-Driver

It was a rainy afternoon when I jumped into a taxi driven by a 48-year-old gentleman named John. I was grateful that he had stopped to pick me up, despite the heavy downpour. In perfect English, he started a conversation with me.

It turns out that he used to be a Manufacturing Director in a plastics mould manufacturer who had travelled the region in Business Class and dined only at the fanciest restaurants. When his company's last factory in Singapore was closed in 2008, he moved to China where he helped set up a friend's factory.

Four years later, he was replaced by a local and he came back to Singapore. He had tried looking for jobs for over 18 months, but nobody wanted to hire him, so he took to driving a taxi to make ends meet. He told me he had an MBA.

In the past 20 years, there has been an unnerving trend that has only recently earned the attention of policy makers in many governments. It is the situation where workers are no longer able to secure jobs that they want simply because there is no longer a need for the skills that they have, or that the experience and knowledge that they possess had expired.

Economists call this condition being *'Unemployable'*.

The Oxford Dictionary defines this as 'the state a person is in where he is unable or unlikely to get paid employment because of a lack of skills or qualifications'.

An obvious symptom of this condition is when an individual has attended numerous interviews for numerous roles but after 6 months, he is still unable to land a role because he doesn't have the right expertise for any current roles in the market. Because of the fast-changing nature of skills demanded, this poses a major threat anywhere in the world, regardless of whether it is a developed or developing country.

In Singapore alone, statistics has shown that up to 50% of those above 50 years old who were retrenched were unable to find jobs for as long as half-a-year after they had lost their jobs.

Being unemployable is bad from a societal standpoint where individuals are chronically unable to find employment.

From a personal standpoint, it is even worse as the individual's self-worth and confidence plummet since our jobs and careers form a large part of our identity.

Alarmingly, it is not only the old or the unskilled who are at risk of being unemployable. Consider the following real-life examples:

The 35-year-old Scientist
(The Niche Specialist)

Thomas was a cancer researcher with a PhD in T-cell Therapeutics. Based in Singapore, he had over 12 years of substantial work experience under his belt when the funding for his project was withdrawn.

Without a research grant, there was no way he could continue his good work. The only other place that carried out research in the same field was in California, USA but he was unable to move because of an elderly parent who was not in good health.

Despite his doctorate, he was unable to find work for over a year because he was so specialized and is presently a part-time science tutor to primary school children.

The 40-year-old Regional Vice President
(The Expensive Executive)

Susan was one of the rising stars in an IT Consulting Firm where she had been since graduation. At 33, she was made a Full Partner and by 38, she was a Regional Vice President who was earning close to $650,000 per year.

The long hours and late-night conference calls, coupled with an exhausting regional travel schedule took its toll on her health and she experienced a bad burnout at 40. She suffered massive weight loss, anxiety, and insomnia and for health reasons, resigned from her company and took a 6-month career break.

When she decided to return to the workforce, she found that nobody wanted to hire her as she was 'too expensive' or 'too senior' for her age. When she tried to go for a smaller role, hiring managers wondered why she was 'settling for less' and wondered if she would stay only until a better offer came along. She has been out a job for over 9 months and is still actively interviewing.

Many employers felt Susan had 'peaked too early' in her career and was simply too expensive to hire.

The 47-year-old Training Manager
(The Muddled Middleman)

Sam was a Learning & Development Manager at an oil company for the past 15 years. Rising through the ranks, he started as a Human Resource Executive and climbed his way to a management role when he was in his mid-30s.

His role was to assess the employees' training needs and appoint vendors to provide the required training. As he was a manager, he no longer conducted any classroom training and because he did not have any specific technical knowledge, he was not qualified to deliver any training. He had little skills to call his own.

He was retrenched last year and is finding himself to be increasingly unemployable.

This is because as the 'middle-man', his contribution to any organization was limited. He couldn't conduct any training, and the role of 'instructional design', which was one of his key functions, was provided by the training agencies themselves. He was no longer needed.

The 52-year-old Loan Officer (The Disrupted Dinosaur)

Vincent was a loan approval officer at a bank. His main job was to assess the creditworthiness of his bank's clients. Managing a team of 8 executives, he had been in this role for the past 18 years.

Last year, the bank offshored this function and retrenched 6 of his staff but kept him on as he was still needed for the handover. The company also automated the loans application process via an Artificial Intelligence software and he received his retrenchment notice 6 months ago.

He tried applying for similar positions in other banks but soon realized that they, too, had automated the process and didn't need such a senior manager in their organization. No jobs were available.

With a diminished demand for his skillset, Vincent is still hopeful that one of the banks might need his experience someday, so he can land a job to pay his mounting bills.

From these real-life examples we have encountered, we realized that unemployability can hit anyone, regardless of age, education level, or performance.

Indeed, unemployability is something we have to strive hard to avoid.

Irreversible Hiring Trends in the Post-Pandemic Era

No one can dispute the fact that Covid-19 has changed the way we work, no matter which part of the globe we are in. From adjusting to working from home to the rise of technological tools that enable effective delivery of quality work without stepping into the office, we have had to embrace these changes, willingly or otherwise.

By themselves, these individual changes present little to moderate risk to the economy, but combined, this confluence could prove a lethal set of body blows to any country's workforce. Let us explain.

The Distance Economy

One thing that Covid-19 lockdowns have demonstrated to employers is that technology has allowed us to truly go global.

Business travel has declined to zero and yet companies have thrived. Technology has enabled businesses to be effectively managed remotely. Face-to-face interactions we once thought indispensable is no longer needed. Workers have come to appreciate Zoom meetings as a better alternative to uncomfortable flights to faraway offices. Some studies even claim that productivity arising from remote work has even improved by up to 13%.

As a result, workers are more than happy to work from home, with a whopping 76% indicating a reluctance to return to the office.[4] Customers are also getting comfortable with service providers that support them virtually rather than in person.

This has created a worldwide acceptance of the 'Distance Economy' where workers do not need to be physically present to get the work done.

Jobs Leakage

Because of the effectiveness of 'work from home', business leaders realized that their staff need not be physically present in the office

---

[4] Islam, Zak, 'Employees don't want to return to the office... but bosses do. Job satisfaction 62% higher for execs', *Techspot*, Oct 6, 2021, https://www. techspot.com/news/91605-employees-dont-want-return-office-but-bosses-do. html#:~:text=A%20whopping%2076%20percent%20of,or%20all%20of%20 the%20time.

to do a good job. In fact, they need not even be in the same country. After all, since work is executed remotely, it makes no difference whether the executive is in Singapore or Manila.

As a result, many companies are starting to relocate roles outside of Singapore, but attaching these teams to the Singapore Regional Headquarters.

An MNC client recently established a Technical Support Centre in Singapore and gave the jobs to a team based in KL on the basis that 'the local team wasn't going to be based in the office anyway'. This resulted in 46% cost-savings for them, with little or no drop in service quality.

Consequently, Singapore is leaking jobs to cheaper locations, and given our high-cost base, it makes good commercial sense for companies to adopt this strategy.

This phenomenon is not just restricted to Singapore, as our counterparts in the US have reported that many jobs that used to be based in expensive New York or San Francisco have moved to cheaper locations in the US heartlands where many workers have gone home—which leads us to the next phenomenon.

The Reverse Brain-Drain

Covid-19 has brought about a peculiar 'reverse brain drain' phenomenon across the region.

Traditionally, the best regional talents were largely based in Singapore, Hong Kong, Shanghai, and Tokyo, the de-facto regional hubs of Asia.

However, because of the Covid-19 lockdowns and mass retrenchments across Asia, many talented business professionals and managers have returned to their countries of origin, bringing home with them their years of expertise where they enjoy both closeness to family and a significantly lower cost of living.

A Malaysian Regional Compensation & Benefits Director who was based in Hong Kong for over 12 years recently repatriated to KL after being retrenched. Undaunted, she hunted for jobs in the region and was recently hired by an American company headquartered in Singapore.

Her asking price was a startling 50% lower than her previous HK package, but when converted to her local currency, she felt that it 'was a princely sum, given the lower running costs at home'. She edged out 3 Singapore-based candidates for that job.

Covid-19 has reversed the talent flight observed in the booming years and has resulted in a growing availability of appropriately qualified and cheaper manpower scattered across less expensive countries around the globe.

This means that competition for plump roles is not limited to candidates from the same city, and in fact, because Covid-19 has accelerated the adoption and acceptance of remote work, there is more competition than before. Employers choose to hire equally qualified candidates from lower cost cities as this would keep headcount costs low.

An Impending Job Apocalypse?

So, given the powerful confluence of the distance economy, jobs leakage and reverse brain drain, we are observing an increase in external competition for in-country jobs.[5]

The frightening truth is that because this supply of external talent is outside the control of governments trying to regulate employment and protect local jobs, there is little the leadership can do to stem the flow.

Once companies realize the presence of cheaper, more qualified talents who can work remotely, it will only be a matter of time before affordable foreign-based talents begin competing for local jobs, making it difficult for individuals to find jobs in their own cities.

---

[5] Berger, Chloe, 'The death of offices and the rise of remote work could mean someone with your title makes 20x more than you', *Fortune*, Feb 25, 2022, https://fortune.com/2022/02/25/could-a-remote-workforce-lead-to-more-income-inequality/.

As a result, we are facing external threats that are beyond our control that require smarter strategies to manage.

Goodbye Career Ladder, Hello Career Lattice

Another major change in the employment landscape is the disappearance of what was traditionally known as a career ladder. Executives who look upwards for their career advancement will find fewer such opportunities as traditional hierarchies are flattened.

'I can't be promoted until my boss resigns, gets promoted or retires' used to be a common refrain with many ambitious executives.

The truth is, the old career ladder model of linear career progression is now dead and executives who think and strategize along this path will find it increasingly difficult to get promoted. A new model of career progression is needed and this comes in the form of a career lattice.

This entails a forward trajectory that need not necessarily be upwards, but could be in the form of a lateral move. For instance, a Sales Director not seeking her boss's role as Sales VP, but rather, her colleague's role as Marketing Director so that she can get wider exposure which would be advantageous in her ambition to become the CEO of the company in the future.

These types of lateral moves are becoming increasingly common and offer a wider range of career options for the executive in the long run.

So, in today's flatter hierarchies, you need to think out of the box to get ahead in your career.

'Life-long Employment' is a Thing of the Past

Gone are the days when an executive would join a company straight out of college, work 30 years with the same company, and retire with a gold watch and a healthy retirement fund. That stereotype is gone. You are in the driver's seat and have to be responsible in navigating and managing your career. Most regular executives would see an average of 8 career changes in a lifetime and side-gigs are becoming a common practice.

In the 'good old days', one of the bigger selling points of joining a large company like say, Shell, was that they would promise you a 'career for life' in the company.

Not anymore.

I recently spoke to the CEO of a US $150 million start-up who said, 'I don't even want to promise my new hires a career with my company—my staff are free to leave me anytime and I'm free to release them if their skills are no longer needed'.

Today, companies have realized that they are no longer obligated to the employees, but rather, to the shareholders. What happened?

Given the breakneck speed of change that today's digital age brings, companies are forced to evolve to continue making profits or become obsolete.

Companies like Nokia, which famously started as a pulp mill in the 19th century, had to switch from making television sets in the '80s—they were the third largest TV manufacturer, after Philips and Thomson—to mobile phones in '90s. When their mobile phone business declined in the mid-2000s, they begun manufacturing and selling network equipment.

Market forces push companies to dream up new products and services, and unfortunately, the older ones will need to be shelved. When a company like Samsung decided that making mobile phones was more profitable than making personal computers, they shut down their PC assembly plants in China and laid off 1700 workers[6], top performers and all. Think about it—we buy new PCs every three years, but new mobile phones almost yearly.

---

[6] 'Samsung Electronics to halt production at its last computer factory in China', Reuters, August 1, 2020, https://www.reuters.com/article/us-samsung-elec-china-pc-idUSKBN24X3K4.

These changes to organization structures in response to competitive pressures result in a continuous wave of retrenchments. As a result, no company is ever immune to it, and hence, everyone's job is at risk.

The harsh reality is that when the company's profits are at risk, it's either your job or the CEO's that has to go, and guess who is the one making all the decisions?

Indeed, in today's context, nobody's job is guaranteed anymore.

The Gig Economy has Arrived

Because there is no longer 'lifelong' employment, we cannot expect to spend our entire careers with a single company. In fact, given the fast-moving nature of the job market, we anticipate having to move every few years either voluntarily (due to better jobs/salaries) or involuntarily (due to corporate downsizing exercises).

In other words, your career is going to be a series of jobs, one after another; or as musicians will call it, a series of gigs.

A gig is defined as a short-term, temporary job with an uncertain future. So, for as much as you *think* you have a job at your company, it is in reality only a gig unless you are being guaranteed a role there until you retire.

Hence there is a need to think of your career not just as a job in a company over many years, but as a series of gigs where you deliver good results at each juncture and then move on to the next one.

There should no longer be any sense of permanence or fealty to the companies you are working with as the organization very likely does not have any plans on keeping you with them forever.

So, if your job is only a temporary gig, shouldn't you be planning for your next gig once this one runs out? Do you know where you will be going or what you will be doing next?

The Shift from Job Market to Skills Market

Many people have been complaining about how tough the job market has been over the past few years where it is getting increasingly difficult to find good jobs that fit their profile. This is because many roles have been evolving but unfortunately, many workers haven't. There has been a growing disconnect between jobs and skills.

Simply having held the post of sales manager may not fully prepare you for the highly specialized skills required by the hiring company to increase market share via a digital sales lead generation strategy.

Hence, there has been a noticeable shift during the job interview from 'What jobs have you been doing?' to 'What skills do you have to offer my company?' or 'How can you solve my specific problem?'

By allowing yourself to be defined by your job description/title rather than by your skills, you are limiting a lot of opportunities that lie just around the corner, out of sight. Conversely, not knowing what your best skills are also restricts your visibility to new and exciting 'out of the box' roles as well.

Because employers are now looking for skills rather than just job titles, do you know what your most marketable and transferable skills are?

Growing Uncertainty over Future Skill Needs

Today's educators worry over what skills to impart to their students that would be relevant in the future[7] as there is little clarity regarding future employment trends in this fast-changing

---

[7] Rainie, Lee, Anderson, Janna, 'The Future of Jobs and Jobs Training', *Pew Research Centre*, May 3, 2017, https://www.pewresearch.org/internet/2017/05/03/the-future-of-jobs-and-jobs-training/.

economy. Barely eight years ago, there were no job titles like 'Social Media Manager', 'Data Visualization Creator', or 'UX Research Designer', so it was almost impossible to train students for those roles. Looking ahead, who knows what strange and exciting new roles will be created in the near future? How do we look beyond the curve and train the students for such opportunities? This uncertainty over 'future skills' is also applicable to today's executive. What skills will the market require from you five years from today? Will your current skills be rendered obsolete by newer technologies like Artificial Intelligence and Machine Learning, or will the demand for them wane and vanish like the need for blacksmiths?

To stay in demand, executives will have to look far ahead into their future and equip themselves with the right set of skills. However, a recent study we conducted showed that up to 53.5% of executives do not know what future skills they need.

This leads to one of today's burning questions—what is the next big thing for your career? What industry or skill will be in such demand that employers will keep knocking at your door, even ten years from now?

There are so many questions to answer, but one thing is clear— there is a need to learn how to spot future trends in your work and upskill accordingly.

This in itself is a skill you will need to learn and master to stay relevant.

Conclusion

At no point in recent history has the world undergone so many changes at one go. The sheer confluence of technology, information, labour flow, and consumer evolution has created a bubbling cauldron of changes, threats, as well as opportunities for us to navigate. If left alone to these environmental forces, our careers would be at the mercy of external factors that we would find difficult to navigate.

However, there is yet another potent force that we will need to contend with—our outdated approaches towards managing our careers—which will be covered in the next chapter.

3

Career Myths We Need to Dispel

'Did you know that Humans only use 10% of their brains? And mother birds will not take care of their young if a person touches the baby bird?'

Since we were children, we have always been taught 'facts' that seem to make sense, but as we grow older, we realized that just because something 'sounds right' doesn't make it true, like the two statements we just read. Humans use a lot more than 10% of their brains[8], and no, birds will still look after their young regardless of who has touched them.[9] So why do we still believe these myths?

Many of us were brought up with our parents and teachers giving us sound career advice. Even today, we are still being counselled by well-meaning friends who wish the best for us by sharing their own opinions on the right types of career decisions to make. However, much of this advice is often based on outmoded

---

[8] Boyd, Robynne, 'Do People Only Use 10 Percent of Their Brains?' *Scientific American*, Feb 7, 2008, https://www.scientificamerican.com/article/do-people-only-use-10-percent-of-their-brains/.

[9] Boyd, Robynne, 'Fact or Fiction?: Birds (and Other Critters) Abandon Their Young at the Slightest Human Touch', Scientific American, July 26, 2007, https://www.scientificamerican.com/article/fact-or-fiction-birds-abandon-young-at-human-touch/.

sets of assumptions that we call 'Careers 1.0 Thinking'; ideas that used to be true, but in today's world, are not true anymore.

The world has changed dramatically and the career challenges that we face need to be handled with a new perspective, something many well-intentioned advisors lack. In the same vein as we would never advise anyone discovering a strange, painless lump in their neck to get treatment advice from their friends or colleagues, we have always advocated getting career advice from the professional career experts because they are aware of today's job market requirements and practices.

Following outdated career advice that are based on career myths could prove detrimental to your career progression if you acted on them.

Here are some of the few career myths we need to dispel.

Study Hard, Work Hard, Be Loyal, Find a Stable Job and Retire.

This is something that has been ingrained deeply into our psyche by our parents and teachers alike.

'Study hard, be a doctor, a lawyer or an engineer!' they admonished. 'These are stable jobs.'

Although it is true that being highly educated opens doors to better-paying jobs, ironically, obtaining advanced degrees in specialized fields could limit your options instead of expanding them.

A client with a PhD lamented the lack of opportunities because she was seen as 'over-qualified'. Facing limited options, she settled on a part-time role as a private tutor.

Even though the quest for higher education and improving oneself makes for good career prospects, getting an MBA or other certifications without understanding how or whether they can benefit your employment prospects could result in a waste of money and time. Thus, one must have a strategy in play.

The second advice—to be a loyal employee—also does not always hold true in today's context.

This outdated pearl of wisdom is constantly challenged as companies today are more focused on short term gain than employee loyalty. We have witnessed many corporate restructuring and retrenchments where headcount was sacrificed at the altar of increased profitability. The truth is that companies no longer feel an obligation of loyalty to their staff and workers need to understand this and be open to external opportunities and be prepared to act on them.

Your Company will take Care of Your Career

Real Career Stories: Joanna, 59, Office Manager

Joanna had worked in her Bank for 35 years. She prided herself as one of the longest serving employees and had even framed her Long-service Awards in her cubicle. Everyone in the office loved her.

One Monday morning, she was called into her HR Manager's office and there was a zoom call that was open for her. It was an unknown Canadian lady who curtly introduced herself as the new HR VP and informed Joanna that her immediate boss in Hong Kong had been retrenched. This came as a shock to her as he, too, had been with the company for almost as long as her. This new HR leader then informed Joanna that as a result of the new structure, she no longer had a role there and was asked to pack up and leave before lunchtime.

Joanna was shocked and burst out crying and walked back to her office flabbergasted. She lamented, 'This is a betrayal! I've given 35 of my best years to this company only to be kicked to the curb. All those late nights I chose work over my social life, all the relationships I gave up because of my busy work commitments have all come to naught. I feel so cheated and this is all their fault!'

In the days before 2000, companies used to design very comprehensive career pathways for their staff. Companies like Shell and GE ensured job rotations, technical training, and overseas attachments for their staff and were part of a structured 'Employee Career Development' program.

Fast forward to today, few companies invest in such developmental programs, and even if they did, it is usually reserved for high-calibre executives displaying high potential—the future leaders they want to groom and develop.

Even though employees often complain about this lack of career development, organizations cannot be faulted when the employee's average tenure is getting increasingly shorter to only 2 to 3 years in recent time.[10] From a company's perspective, it seems like a futile task to invest in workers who have no qualms about leaving for better paying jobs.

As such, organizations cannot and will not be able to manage their employees' careers; therefore, executives like yourself will have to take charge of your own careers and not play a passive role in charting your own future within your company or with another.

One cannot simply rely on the company to plan your career—you must take responsibility for your own career development.

Follow Your Passion

The road to hell is indeed paved with good intentions and it is true that a dull knife is more dangerous than a sharp one. Often, poor advice comes from well-meaning but unqualified individuals wanting to help you.

One of the worst pieces of advice we often hear is 'You have to follow your passion'. Whilst following your passion is not always a

---

[10] Tacadena, Gerv, 'Job security becoming less important for Singaporean millennials', *Singapore Business Review*, 2017, https://sbr.com.sg/hr-education/in-focus/job-security-becoming-less-important-singaporean-millennials.

bad thing, it is the blind pursuit of this passion to the exclusion of all reality that is dangerous.

We had a client who quit her lucrative banking job to start a bakery because some friends told her that her muffins were 'world-class'. So, she quit her job, invested thousands into a bakery, only to discover how much work was involved and had to shut it down a year later.

Instead of following the advice of her friends, she should have conducted more market research, spoken to other bakers who have similarly pivoted, just to get a better idea of the market instead of making a hasty move based on passion alone. In the high-risk world of today, there is a need to balance passion with practicality.

Your Job Must have Meaning and Purpose

Books like *The Purpose-driven Life* and *Know Your Why* have increased awareness of the need for meaning in the things people do. These books preach the philosophy that life without a cause leading to a sense of fulfilment would not be rewarding. Hence, we know of people who grow frustrated with their jobs because they feel it is 'not rewarding enough to their soul'. They feel unfulfilled at work because their careers are unable to fill their need to 'do good' or to give them purpose and meaning in life.

A client of ours—a finance manager in charge of balancing the monthly accounting for a logistic company—confided in us, saying 'This is a meaningless job that does not give me any inner satisfaction. The work is mundane and repetitive, and at times, I really do not know how I am even making a difference to the world. I need to look for a new one where I can feel better about my mindless work'.

However, when she spoke to us, we highlighted to her that her company provides medical equipment to hospitals and patients in the region, so her contribution at work actually helps countless people in their moment of need. Upon hearing this, she changed her mind about leaving her company.

Some people also forget that they have a life outside of the office, and they can find purpose and meaning there. We know many individuals who find self-fulfillment and personal achievements doing activities on weekends like volunteering at soup kitchens, or engaging in hobbies like painting or gardening.

The myths that you must find meaning in your work and that you can only find fulfilment at the office have led many to leave their good jobs in search of more 'meaningful work', only to find disappointment again.

The Illusion of Job Security

A bird perches on the branches of a tall tree peacefully not because of its faith in the strength of the branch, but rather because of its confidence in the strength of its wings. If the bough breaks, it simply flies off to the next tree.

Unlike our confident little bird, many people worry about job security, wondering whether the company will keep them on payroll and for how long.

In a recent study conducted by us, 78.1% of employees above the age of 45 indicated that they were concerned about job security. They were unsure whether they would still have a job in 12 months' time and looked to their companies for assurance.

In today's uncertain job market, where retrenchment numbers remain high, these fears are not unfounded.

A senior manager we met once confessed that his fear of losing his job was so great, he resorted to using office politics to get ahead of his colleagues in an attempt to be the last man standing. He even tried leveraging his internal connections to try get an internal transfer to a more stable position.

However, executives today need to realize that the myth of job security is only an illusion as everybody's job is at risk. Such short-term fixes will not solve their longer-term challenges of remaining employed.

Executives should instead be focusing on career security, where they are ensured continued employment because they have the skills, the knowledge, and the expertise that continue to be in demand, regardless of whichever company they join. Like the bird sitting on the tall tree, they should be confident in their own ability to find better jobs themselves, rather than depending on their bosses to keep providing employment to them.

Conclusion

There are many beliefs that are ingrained in us that no longer hold any water. From outdated perceptions to well-intentioned career advice, we need to discard fallacious ideas as they could affect our careers negatively. Blindly adhering to them could derail your career, leading to career suicide. Therefore, we need an alternative model for our new-found career thinking: a strategy incorporating the dynamic nature of work with a forward-looking approach which will weather the storms into the 2030s and beyond.

After years of in-depth research, we believe that we have discovered a career model that works. This is what we will share with you over the next few chapters.

Part C

Crafting a New Model

4

'So How?'—The Career Agility Model

'How do you eat an elephant, Daddy?' the little girl asked cheekily.
'I don't know, Honey. How do you eat an elephant?'
the father enquired.
'One piece at a time, Daddy! One piece at a time!'
smiled the little angel.

As we have seen in the previous sections, because of the constantly shifting equilibrium of the working world and the outdated thinking that many of us still harbour, many of us are under threat of becoming irrelevant in the employment market. To adapt, we need to craft and develop a new model. This new model has to take into account the ever-shifting sands of technology, globalization, and skills demand and supply in a market that is evolving at a ground-breaking pace.

After countless discussions with hundreds of thought leaders and senior business leaders, we have developed a new framework called 'The Career Agility Model' which can act as a master strategy on which individuals can base their major career decisions on.

But before any framework can be developed, we must always begin with the end in mind. What exactly are the major outcomes in our careers that we hope to achieve with this model? What are the overriding goals of every career plan that we come up with?

Many have been suggested 'wealth building', 'legacy building', and even 'accelerating in the shortest time'. However, we feel that the universal goals should be just that—'universal' and appealing to all individuals, and must be valued by all, in the simplest form possible.

As such, our 'Career Agility Model' strives to achieve two goals.

The first objective is Career Longevity

Definition:
Career Longevity: Having a sustainable career by continually being in demand by employers until the day you **choose** to exit the job market.

Famed neuroscientist and author David Levitin recently said, 'The new retirement age is . . . NEVER'.[11] Firstly, given the modern person's life expectancy of 82 years, it seems inconceivable for most people to retire or stop working at 62 and have enough money to support them for the next 20 years of their life.

---

[11] Letvin, Daniel, What is the ideal age to retire? Never, according to a neuroscientist, *TED*, Feb 27, 2020, https://ideas.ted.com/what-is-the-ideal-age-to-retire-never-according-to-a-neuroscientist/.

With ongoing bills to pay, many would have to continue working well into their late 60s or early 70s just to pay off their mortgages!

More importantly, even for those who can afford to retire at 62 or earlier, it is highly unlikely that every single one of them would desire to sit at home and do absolutely nothing for the next two decades. This sedentary and unstimulating lifestyle could lead to unhealthy outcomes for many.

Other workers we have spoken to—who are nearing their retirement age—have shared that they still hope to be productive and are able to find work they love doing and continue contributing to society. So, it seems that the concept of retirement has changed from a time when it meant dropping out of the workforce entirely to do nothing at age 55 to staying economically active in a format that may or may not conform to a full-time employment model.

Thus, those wishing to continue working beyond the official retirement age need to consider this. They must ensure that there will always be some demand for the work or services that they can provide so they can continue to stay employed until the day they wish to exit the market.

In other words, we need to strive to ensure career longevity by avoiding unemployability.

As highlighted in Chapter 2, the threat of being unemployable is becoming increasingly real, regardless of one's seniority, role, or industry.

For example, a factory manager could find his work being exported to cheaper locations where he would not want to relocate to. Or a high-flying senior vice-president could find his lucrative salary becoming too large an expense for his company to bear and is suddenly priced out of the market.

The truth is that while the state of being unemployed can be quickly fixed, the state of being unemployable could prove to be chronic and, occasionally, terminal.

The second objective is Career Satisfaction

Why do we drag ourselves out of bed every morning, dress up, and spend the next 9 hours at work every day? Is it just to get a pay cheque? Is it just to be with friendly colleagues? Or is it to do meaningful work?

It is not enough to have a long and sustainable career without enjoying what you do. In fact, it would be pointless to be in a job you hate or are bored with, year after year!

So, the second objective of career planning is to be in a role where you are enjoying yourself and are achieving career satisfaction.

We have deliberately chosen the word 'Career Satisfaction' over 'career happiness' because it is impossible to be in a constant state of happiness even if you are in a great job as there will always be tough days at work. We did not want to create an unrealistic expectation of being happy all the time.

From our extensive research and discussions, we found that one of the reasons behind career satisfaction is achieving career success. However, what exactly does career success mean to you?

What is Career Success?

We like asking everyone we meet what they want in life, and the common refrain is always, 'I want to be happy!' And they are absolutely correct.

However, our happiness is influenced by many elements, for instance, family, friends, money, health, hobbies, relationships, a good night's sleep, and more!

- Family
- Friends
- Money
- Health

Personal Happiness

- Hobbies
- Religion
- Sleep
- Relationships

Real Career Story: Jane, Regional Director, 46

'I want a job with less travel so I can spend more time with my children. I've been on the road 70% of my time my entire career and my eldest daughter, now 18 and studying in Australia, is a stranger to me. My son who's 10, cried when I told him I was flying off for another 2-week business trip. My heart broke. This job isn't worth it. Can you find me a better one? I don't mind taking a pay cut.'

We managed to present her a role that was only 20% travel but had a corresponding $8,000/month decrease in salary (from her current salary of $35,000/month).

She looked at the number and hesitated. 'Can they throw in a better company car? I don't want to downgrade from my Mercedes!'

I told her the client had a budget that they had to adhere to and after much thought, she declined the role.

'The money and the car just isn't worth it,' she declared.

'What about your son?' I reminded her.

She looked at me and replied, 'Well, I guess he just has to make do'.

I sighed and reserved my judgement. That day, I realized that different people had different definitions of 'success'.

All these things affect our everyday level of happiness and play an important role in our general well-being. However, one major area that affects our happiness—which is often overlooked when we ask our clients—is 'Career Success'.

Our careers play a very important role in our lives as we spend more than half our waking hours at work or thinking about work. Being successful in our careers can bring us many benefits. Besides money, it brings us pride, satisfaction, joy, purpose, etc. In fact, just as having a successful career brings us happiness that will in turn affect factors like our health, family relationships and finances, having a troubled career will adversely affect these as well.

For example, when you have experienced a good day at work, you bring home the positivity and cheer that will filter into your relationships. Conversely, if you hate your job or your toxic colleagues, the negativity that surrounds you will inevitably infect the way you relate to your loved ones. As we can see, career success affects and influences a person's level of happiness and we should always strive to attain it.

But what constitutes 'Career Success'?

When asked what defines career success, our clients gave a huge range of responses. These are the top six.

We can clearly see that many factors contribute to career success. You will notice that not every factor applies to you; you might value work-life balance but not the corner office. These choices are highly personal and there are no right or wrong answers.

This highlights the fact that different people have different ideas of what career success means to them. In fact, even for the same person, the definition of career success changes throughout their life. For instance, a young graduate starting out in life might place high value on salary and learning new skills, whereas someone in his 40s with young children might value job stability more, whilst a 52-year-old would probably value work-life balance to spend time with their loved ones.

So, the relationship between personal happiness and career success is very closely connected, with one affecting and influencing the other. Putting it all together, the model looks like this:

As you can see from the above chart, your 'career success' (or the lack of it) can—and will—affect your personal happiness and vice versa.

So, the question that is often asked is, 'Why are people with seemingly successful careers and flaunting their big flashy cars still unhappy in their lives?'

The reason is simple.

They are pursuing the types of career successes they *think* that society measures them by. They work hard to achieve a high-flying career, a fancy job-title and the prized corner office. However, they don't realize that these are not what they truly want in life. Hence they get burnt out trying to impress those who really shouldn't matter to them.

So, in order for you to achieve your personal vision of career success, you need to step back and reflect. What does Career Success really look like to you? Is it being able to afford nice things or going on a luxury vacation with your family? Or is it being able to give back to society? Could it be getting recognition for your wonderful ideas or achievements? Or is it simply being able to enjoy a peaceful night's sleep?

Understand what career success means to you and drive towards these goals. Do not bother about what your friends, neighbours, or peers are pursuing or have achieved. Exercise the wisdom to focus on what is important to you and work towards it. Only then can you truly find personal happiness in life.

Real Career Story: Cynthia, Management Consultant, 35

She was always the top student in her class and academic excellence always came easy for her. Marked as a 'genius' from age 5, she memorized the periodic table at age 7 and had the top universities knocking on her door at 18.

She received a full scholarship to an Ivy League University and graduated the top of her class and joined a prestigious management consulting group which sponsored her Harvard MBA.

She was fast-tracked to partner and was jet-setting her way around the world, moving from one high profile project to the next. She spent so much time travelling that she felt she was living out of hotels and airport lounges.

'I was switched on at 150 miles per hour from the time I woke up until I shut my eyes, getting only 5 hours of sleep a day. And I loved that!'

This was until one morning when she woke up with a bad migraine that didn't go away for days. Her body was telling her that she had to slow down. She was experiencing a case of burnout.

She flew home and let her parents take care of her for 2 weeks as she recuperated and she realized that all the hard work and abuse she had put her mind and body through was not worth it.

She resigned that following week and started to re-evaluate what was most important to her at that point in her life.

Conclusion

So, in order to attain personal happiness, we need to strive towards achieving career successes that matter to us as well as ensuring career longevity by remaining employable. This involves knowing the most meaningful career success factors to pursue and achieve as well as understanding what your skills and expertise are and where the demand is coming from.

However, these two goals do not materialize easily by themselves and you will need 2 essential components to make this happen: a **Career Strategy** to plan the next moves forward, and the **Career Agility** to power your plan into action. We will take a closer look at both over the next two chapters.

5

Career Strategy

How much is your career worth to you today? If you knew the total monetary value attached to the earning capacity of the rest of your economic life, would your view on your career change?

The truth is that there is a way you can estimate the value of your future career and the results may surprise you and force you to rethink your career in a radically different way. Let's look at the math.

As with all financial calculations involving time and money, we use the traditional NPV (Net Present Value) model which helps define how much future income-flows are of value to us today. To find your Career NPV, simply multiply your current annual salary with the number of working years remaining, then multiplying it with a 'growth factor' which represents the rate at which your career grows (or declines).

It could be represented mathematically as follows:

Career NPV (Net Present Value)	= Annual salary	× Number of working years remaining	× Growth factor

Say, a 35-year-old finance manager earns $100,000 per year and intends to work until she is 55. Assuming she stays in her company and enjoys a 3% increase in her salary every year, her calculation would be as follows:

Career NPV = $100,000 × 20 years × 1.03%
(Net Present
Value)
           = $2,687,038

This means that, theoretically, her career is worth almost $2.7 million to her today.

However, there are several assumptions in this model.

Assumption 1: We made a huge assumption that her career will be in a steady state and that there will be no disruptions like a retrenchment where she might be out of a job for months or even a year, leading to a monetary 'gap' in the calculation.

Assumption 2: We assumed that there is no 'step increase' in her salary, like the kind that comes from switching jobs or getting promoted. There is also the implicit assumption that there are no pay cuts due to economic hardships faced by the company.

So, do a quick calculation of your career NPV and see how much your career is worth to you today. With such a large and precious asset, wouldn't you want to figure out a way to preserve it? Wouldn't you want to find methods to avoid it being devalued? Wouldn't it be rewarding to discover ways to tweak that growth factor into a higher ratio and accelerate your career NPV?

You can do all that with a Career Strategy. We need to start treating our careers like a business asset, replete with business plans, contingencies, growth projections, and even an exit strategy, because as cliched as it sounds, if you fail to plan, you plan to fail.

What is Career Strategy and how do you develop it?

We all have strategies for any project we work on. When launching a new product, we ask ourselves,

- How do we price it?
- What is the message behind it?
- When should we launch it?
- How do we handle our competitors' response to it?

We have mental models for the work-related aspect of our life as well as our own personal areas of decision-making process. We have diet strategies to ensure we eat healthily. We have investment strategies so that we get the maximum yield on our hard-earned cash. We have an exercise-strategy so that we can have optimal results for our hard work at the gym.

So, we are often perplexed to discover that so many executives out there in the market do not have a Career Strategy!

As career experts, we have studied the careers of various business leaders and have noted that there is one common thread among those who have been successful in their careers. They all had a Career Strategy. They had a well-laid plan which they had developed and adhered closely to. They had a vision and seemed to know what they were doing. On the other hand, executives who had neither the time nor the foresight to develop their own career strategies find themselves derailed when negative events or unexpected opportunities appear on their horizon. For example, they have no idea whether they want to be in the same industry or role 5 years from now and would rather not think about it unless something drastic happens which forces their hand. However, things might be too late by then.

Like the Manager of a magazine publishing company who hasn't realized (or refuses to accept) the fact that online consumption of content will render his glossy magazines obsolete but keeps pushing on quarter after quarter anyway.

Often, executives only think about their Career Strategy when they are facing retrenchment or after they have received their pink slip, which is a little too late.

Your Career Strategy should be a living document that is constantly updated and upgraded as you progress along your career journey. With a coherent Career Strategy to guide your path, navigating obstacles and seizing long-term advantages becomes clearer and the way forward is easier. A Career Strategy is a plan you develop based on self-knowledge and market trends, identifying your strengths, weaknesses, passion, and values, as well as various market opportunities and threats looming over your horizon. Your Career Strategy is about self-discovery and should provide a roadmap of where you would like to be years from now and how you are going to get there.

Why have a Career Strategy?

Imagine that you are going on a holiday to Spain. Would you decide to rush to the airline counter at the airport, buy an air ticket for the next plane to Madrid, land there, then decide what you want to see?

Probably not.

Many of us would plan meticulously for a big holiday like that. We would decide which places we want to go to, whether it is a shopping trip, an eating odyssey, or an outdoor/nature adventure, and allocate sufficient time for it. We would have a very well-planned itinerary which will help our daily decisions so we don't deviate from it.

Likewise, having a Career Strategy will enable us to have a roadmap for our future, based on which facts can be referenced and rational decisions made. Moreover, in today's highly disruptive world where old business models are destroyed overnight and new ones created, the high degree of uncertainty makes it even more important to have a set of guideposts that can help us with our contingency planning. Therefore, it is critical that we have a working Career Strategy to guide us along our career journey so that we can make the best decisions.

Real Career Story: Jack Welch, former CEO of General Electric

Jack Welch is the famous CEO who grew the General Electric Company from a US $26.8 billion entity when he took over as CEO in 1980 to a US $130 billion mega-corporation in 2000 when he left.

But did you know that Jack was actually 'Dr Jack Welch'? He had earned a Masters and a PhD in Chemical Engineering from the University of Illinois in 1960, a year before he joined GE.

Jack shared in his book *Jack: Straight From The Gut* that he had deliberately kept that fact a secret from others in the company when he signed up because he had a very clear Career Strategy. He realized that if everyone called him 'Dr Jack', he would be positioned (at a very early stage of his career) on a 'technical/engineering track', rather than on a 'management track' which was what he knew he wanted.

He had the foresight to know that his career options would be very limited if people thought of him as an engineer rather than a manager. Because of this Career Strategy, he was placed on the Management Development Program, instead of the engineering one and he immediately knew his outcomes would be far more promising.

So, he insisted, 'Just call me Jack!' And the rest, as they say, is history!

How to develop my Career Strategy?

Developing your own Career Strategy is not difficult. We recommend that you seek an experienced career advisor to help evaluate your options.

There are two types of career advisors. The first would be a mentor who is a senior or retired business Leader who has had an illustrious career in either your industry or your function.

If you are a finance manager, then, a Chief Finance Officer of a large company would be ideal as a mentor, since this senior executive would possess the wisdom of experience and understand the nuances of your industry. Usually, this could be your former boss.

The other type of career advisor would be a career coach who can help you with your Career Strategy, mapping out your immediate and future career roadmap based on an in-depth understanding of your profile after several meetings with you. Depending on your immediate and long-term needs, they can help with insights and actionable steps on how you can achieve career longevity and career satisfaction.

However, if you would like to take a self-help approach, you can use our 5-Step Career Strategy Framework detailed in the next chapter.

6

The 5-Step Career Strategy Framework

'Before anything else, preparation is the key to success.'
                                        —*Alexander Graham Bell*

In order to create a working Career Strategy, we have developed a
5-step framework that you can use as a map to chart your next steps.

1. Think Long Term

2. Determine Your Career Direction

3. Decide on Your Career Velocity

4. Determine Your Career Intent

5. Understand Your Market

Step 1: Think Long Term

When asked about their career plans, many executives are only thinking about their 'next move' but lose sight of the bigger picture—their long-term career goal. They ask themselves, 'What would I like to do for my next job?', thinking only about job titles and salaries. As a result, they gain short term benefits but sacrifice long term gains.

We often ascribe this career short-sightedness to the need for immediate gratification. When there are bills that need to be paid and hungry mouths to be fed, it is understandably tempting to solve one's near-term problems first. However, we always encourage our clients to imagine themselves 5 years from now, looking back at the present day and asking themselves, 'Was that a wise move to make?'. They should adopt a longer-term view of their career and think about the future role they envision themselves in, 7-10 years from now. This could be two or even three jobs down the road.

By doing so, they can identify gaps in skills and expertise, and can look for jobs or projects that can provide that kind of exposure. For example, if a finance manager wanted to be a CEO to achieve his career goal, he should be trying to land a general manager or sales position to get experience in strategy and business development, rather than the obvious next step as CFO.

A useful exercise when developing your Career Strategy is to ask yourself these difficult questions:

- Where do you want to be 7-10 years from today?
- What are the skills and experience that you need to have to make that vision a reality?
- Will the role provide you with the exposure needed to fill those gaps?
- Will this role make sense in the bigger scheme of things?

With a Career Strategy that answers these questions, selecting the path to your next role or roles will be a lot clearer as you would have the right information needed to make better decisions.

Real Life Career Stories: Robert, Petrochemical Engineer, 40
Robert spent the last 2 decades of his life on oil rigs in distant oceans and on oil fields of countries he could not even locate on a map.

The going was rough and he made a lot of money in his youth, but it was a young man's work and he was afraid that if he carried on in this dangerous field, he might slip up and end up injured or dead.

He knew oilfield engineering was not going to be sustainable for him in the long run and wanted to pivot out into another industry and role that was safer and closer to home, now that his parents were getting older.

He was contemplating teaching engineering at a local polytechnic when a call from an old colleague came.

It was a lucrative job offer for a 3-year project in Azerbaijan and the money was very tempting.

He was at a career crossroad—should he take the short-term monetary gain but risk returning home to face possible unemployability? Or should he spend his next years in academia, pivoting into a new industry that has far greater career longevity?

Step 2: Know Your Career Direction
(Career Quadrants)

For many executives today who feel frustrated in their current role, one of the most difficult questions to answer would be, 'In which direction do I head? Where do I go next? Do I join a competitor, or do I want to make a career switch to something entirely different?'

Ironically, this lack of clarity would result in 'analysis paralysis' that becomes one of the biggest obstacles to making any career move at all. Amidst all the choices and options, the inertia to remain in one place can be overwhelming. We always believe in knowing and framing your options so that you limit your choices to a narrow range of options, rather than eating the entire proverbial elephant at one go. To better understand your career direction, we have developed the Crossover Quadrant Model that simplifies your decision-making into 4 broad options.

The Crossover Quadrants Model

Instead of thinking of the numerous permutations that the next move could entail, we have simplified the options along two dimensions—a change in industry and a change in role.

a. A Change in Industry

When executives think about their next steps, they can decide to stay in the same industry or move to a different one. There are various reasons why anyone might think about switching industries. They could be bored with the industry because they feel they have been there for far too long and want to try something new, or perhaps they prefer going into an industry that promises better growth prospects.

A client who was a project manager in enterprise software implementation had an epiphany and decided that he no longer wanted to eat meat for ethical reasons. He began exploring opportunities in plant-based food industries and managed to land a role with a leading alternative meat company.

He carried on in the same role of software implementation but switched to an entirely different industry successfully.

b. A Change in Role

Another scenario could involve executives who have been in a particular function for too long and have become bored with the same work they have been doing. This could be because they have mastered all the skills needed to get the job done and there is nothing new to learn. They believe that a new role will refresh their skills and rekindle the excitement that they once had for their work.

Our client was a successful sales director of a large hotel group. After twenty years of extensive sales experience, driving revenues across the region, and training her sales team, she no longer felt challenged by that role and wanted to do something different. In 2018, she leveraged her training experience and transferred to her company's Learning and Development Group and became their Chief Sales Trainer.

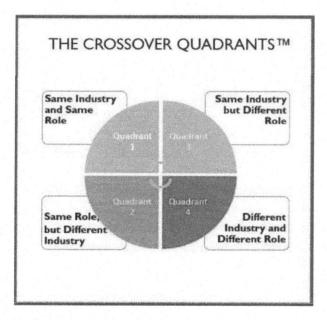

Putting these two dimensions together when considering options, what we get are four combinations as represented in this picture. We call this model the Crossover Quadrant model.

With this model, your next career moves now fall broadly into four categories, each of which we assigned to a quadrant.

Now, let us look at each of these four quadrants in greater detail and what each move entails.

Quadrant 1: Staying in the Same Industry and Same Role

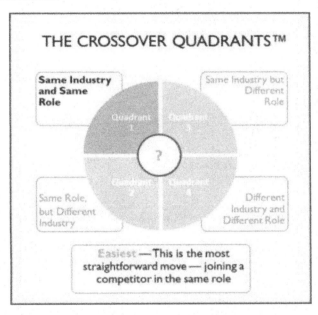

THE CROSSOVER QUADRANTS™

Same Industry and Same Role

Same Industry but Different Role

Same Role, but Different Industry

Different Industry and Different Role

Easiest —This is the most straightforward move — joining a competitor in the same role

Quadrant 1 is also known as the 'join a competitor' move.

Because you are staying in the same industry and within the same role, you are effectively walking across the street to join a competitor in the same or similar industry, in the same or similar role.

For example, a finance manager in an insurance company resigns to join her competitor, a rival insurance company as their finance director.

This move is usually the most straightforward to make, and if you are in an urgent need of a job change, it would probably be the fastest option for you because you are familiar with both the domain and you probably already have all the skills needed to get the job done.

Quadrant 2: Moving to a Different Industry but Staying in the Same Role

Quadrant 2 is also known as the 'switching industries' move.

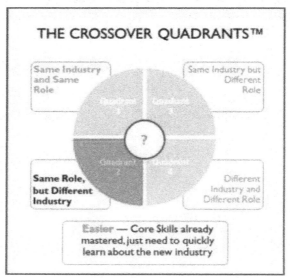

For executives who enjoy their work, they may wish to stay in the same job function but switch to a different industry for better exposure or growth prospects.

For instance, the finance manager in our previous example might consider joining another company in the pharmaceutical sector as their finance manager. Because there is a huge degree of transferability of finance skills and knowledge, it would be an easy switch for her.

Quadrant 3: Staying in the Same Industry but Moving to a Different Role

Quadrant 3 is also known as the 'switching roles' move.

In this case, executives might feel that after having spent years in an industry, they are still quite passionate about it and see further opportunities for growth, but in a different role.

Leveraging their depth of experiences and industry knowledge, their learning curve would be considerably shortened and they can transition quickly into their new role.

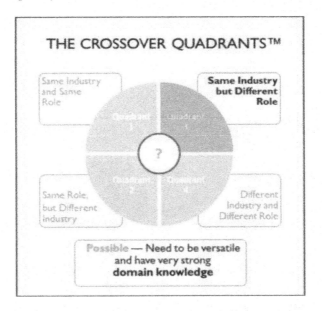

For example, the same finance manager from the previous example who spent years in the insurance industry may decide to join a competing insurance company as their New Product Development Director. In this role, she leverages her knowledge and experience of having analyzed the profitability of various products and her deep understanding of the historical and future demand to craft newer and even more exciting products that the new company could market.

In essence what she has done is that she has stayed within the insurance industry but managed to find a new lease of life in a different role.

Quadrant 4: Moving to a Different Industry and Role

This move is also known as the 'total career switch'.

It involves switching both the role and the industry at the same time, and is often seen to be the riskiest move because you have to learn everything from scratch.

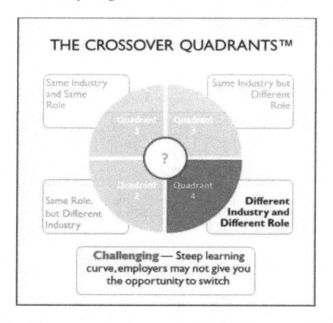

Though not impossible, this move is fraught with many unseen risks, and without proper planning or strategy, it could be really difficult to execute.

We have seen many executives who feel so frustrated at their lack of clear career options that they make a hasty venture into an area that is foreign to them.

For example, our finance manager could wake up one morning and decide to start a bakery because a friend mentioned that her cakes were tasty. Obviously, without any experience in running a bakery, she is likely to face many obstacles and challenges, even potentially losing her entire investment. If you are considering a similar move, we recommend that you spend more time thinking and planning.

Real Career Story: Mike, Accountant, 35

Mike was your typical accountant. He joined a big accountancy firm when he graduated and after 5 years in that company, he left to join a competitor because the pay was better.

He spent another 7 years there as an auditor and at age 35, he was beginning to feel frustrated. 'It's the same boring thing day after day. I can't imagine myself in this role anymore and I want something better,' he confided.

When probed what this 'something better' was, Mike was unable to articulate it. 'I don't know what I want, but I just know I don't want this. I want something different, but I don't know where to begin my job search because the canvas is just too wide. If only there was a way to get clarity and narrow the search parameters to something more manageable so I can focus on particular industries, roles, and companies.'

We introduced the Crossover Quadrants model to him and he realized that he wanted to make a Quadrant 2 move—into the same role, but with a different industry. He decided that being an auditor in the healthcare sector would give his work more meaning and started looking for roles specific to that market.

Within 3 months, he landed a job with a US drug manufacturer and has been very happy since.

Step 3: Determining Your Career Velocity

After deciding which Crossover Quadrant you intend to move into, you will have to figure out your career velocity next.

In physics, velocity is defined as the 'change in displacement of an object in a specific direction'.

On the career front, velocity is defined as how fast you wish to progress the next phase of your career.

There are 5 general vectors that you can consider in this aspect.

Accelerate

Up-and-coming executives who feel that they are ready for career acceleration, this is definitely the option for them.

In search of higher pay, better career prospects, fancy job titles, and wider regional coverage, executives in acceleration mode will drive themselves harder to achieve all this.

However, in today's context, acceleration need not come in the form of only bigger salaries or larger job titles.

Because of the nature of today's organizations' hierarchy, career acceleration need not mean an upward climb into your bosses' role. Instead, it could mean an expansion of skill sets, a deepening of expertise in a particular domain of field, or acquiring new knowledge in high growth areas. This may or may not entail an upgrade in remuneration or designation.

If you are thinking of acceleration as your next strategy forward, you also need to be mindful of the cost that could be involved in engaging such a move. There is always a price you need to pay for something that you want to get.

For instance, having an expanded job scope with wider regional coverage could mean longer hours at work, increased stress due to the higher workload, and less time spent with the family. Are you ready to pay the price? Is your family ready to support you as you make those sacrifices?

A client of ours who was already the marketing director for Asia Pacific took on a global role as the Chief Marketing Officer for the entire company. This meant that he had to manage all aspects of the business worldwide, covering all time zones. This resulted in him having to be available almost 24 hours a day, which ultimately took a toll on his health, and he had to learn how to delegate and manage the business better.

So, there are many considerations to think about if you wish to accelerate your career.

Hover

Some individuals might feel that acceleration is not the right option for them due to personal or professional reasons where they prefer a role that is not too taxing for them.

For example, new parents may wish to limit their travelling schedule and might decline a larger regional portfolio.

Others may decide to 'hover' and maintain a degree of status quo while they decide their next actual career move.

One of the concerns many executives have is the fear that if they took on a lateral move into another company, future employers might question their motivation or perceived lack of ambition.

If you decide to hover, you will need to plan how long you wish to remain in place and what your next steps are and not get complacent in your comfort zone.

Real Career Story: Jacob, Supply Chain Manager, 36

Jacob was a high-flyer in his company and everyone expected him to be the managing director before he turned 42. That meant that he was up for a promotion shortly and everybody was rooting for him.

However, he felt that he was not ready for it yet and needed some time to sort his own Career Strategy out. Moreover, he always wanted to do his MBA before he turned 40. He felt tremendous pressure by his colleagues to accept that promotion, knowing he wouldn't have the time to do both.

Ultimately, he decided to put the promotion on hold and carry on in his current role, whilst signing up for his 2-year part time MBA program. Thankfully, his bosses were supportive of his decision and even sponsored his program.

Downshift

Downshift

Downshifting involves a deliberate reduction of the scale and scope of your work. It is basically a planned move to slow down your career and commonly used by those planning to enter retirement or in preparation for a Portfolio Career, which is discussed in greater detail in Chapter 10.

People downshift for many reasons. You should ask yourself if the real reasons for downshifting are valid or whether they are temporary because this is a major career move to execute.

If you are feeling burnt out because of the intense pace and volume of work, you need to ask yourself if this load is cyclical or permanent. Deciding to downshift because of something that would improve in a few weeks or months could be a bit hasty.

Downshifting could be permanent or temporary.

Many have decided to do a temporary downshift whilst looking after a sick parent or managing a child's major exam, only to jump back into the rat race when things return to normal.

When considering this move, you will also need to plan how long you wish to stay in this mode because reintegrating back into the corporate world at your previous level of seniority gets more challenging with time.

Downshifting is a move to make when there has been, or will be, a significant change in life situation. The reduction in time spent at work will allow more energy to be focused elsewhere.

Real Career Story: Jonas, CFO, 53

It was a particularly tiring quarter for Jonas who was the regional chief finance officer for Asia. Because of a major acquisition, he had been called into global zoom calls at the most unearthly hours and was exposed to the worst politics he had seen in his life. 'I didn't sign up for this,' he shared.

After a tiring 2 a.m. zoom call with the US team on a Saturday morning, he felt he had enough. He recalculated his finances and realized that he actually had more than enough invested to retire comfortably. So, the following Monday, he resigned.

He was very steadfast in wanting a job that was far less stressful and really didn't need much money, so he joined a charity as their internal auditor, earning less than $4,000 a month. He didn't mind the drop in salary as that meant it was a simple job where he could go home every day at 5 p.m. to exercise and spend time with his wife. Over the years, the CEO tried to promote Jonas to finance director but he resolutely refused to take anything that would take his leisure time away from him.

'At my life-stage, the "currency" that is of value to me is not money, but time. It also helps that I'm doing great work for our beneficiaries as it makes my job more meaningful and I go to work every morning with a bounce in my step. I'm glad I downshifted permanently.'

Pause

Sometimes, the workload can get too heavy or the pace, too frenetic and individuals may need to hit that 'pause button' to re-evaluate their options. This could be in the form of a short-term vacation or a longer-term sabbatical.

It is unfortunate that in a pandemic-hit environment where working from home (WFH) is now the norm, many workers are not utilizing their annual leave.[12]

This could lead to burnout and employee exhaustion, and many mid-level executives have already reported higher levels of work stress as a result.

That is why a good strategy to use is to take a break. Even a short 3 days 'personal time out' where the executive is disconnected from office technology to catch up on his/her sleep can prove effective.

---

[12] Dickler, Jessica, 'The year is over and workers left almost all of their vacation days on the table', *CNBC*, Dec 31, 2020, https://www.cnbc.com/2020/12/31/this-is-what-happens-to-all-those-vacation-days-that-never-got-used.html.

Taking a temporary pause to reconsider your options, or to recover from a difficult work experience, or to take care of an ill family member is becoming more acceptable these days and is not uncommon anymore.

Real Career Story: Karen, 39, Logistics Manager

'This happened to me 6 years ago. I found that the routine work that I did was quite meaningless and unrewarding. I was basically filing paperwork all day long and it was getting mundane and tiring. I had been working at that company for 8 years.

One day, at age thirty-three, I got so frustrated that I just resigned with no job in hand. I quit, traded all my leave against the mandated notice period, and walked out of the office. That weekend, I packed my bags, jumped on a plane to the Sunshine Coast in Australia, and crashed at a friend's place for the next three months.

I spent the days by the beach 'decompressing' and pondering my next moves. I managed to spend time with my old friends there and even visited some long-lost relatives. Feeling recharged towards the end of my getaway there, I decided that my mini-sabbatical was over, and it was time for me to find another job. I returned home renewed and recharged, and landed an exciting role with a global logistics company and have been there since. The 'pause' put some sanity back into my life.

There are no right or wrong career velocity strategies to take.

A promising 30-year-old might decide to downshift and a 60-year-old might decide to accelerate. Every decision is personal and depends on individual circumstances and thinking, so there should not be any moral judgement around this.

Exit

For many, retirement is the end-game. Or is it?

There was a time not too far back when the mandatory retirement age was 55. Today, this age feels much too early to drop all your tools to ride off into the sunset.

Globally, the retirement age ranges from 62–67 which to many, can seem like a long time away and that there is no need to plan for it today.

Nonetheless, if you are planning for such exit, you will probably need to think of how you can remain mentally engaged, either economically to the workforce or socially with the people around you, and what you can do today to help facilitate that.

In summary, understanding your career velocity, i.e., how fast you wish your career to progress, is important because it will help determine your next course of action, the type of jobs you wish to seek, and even the format of work you wish to engage in.

Real Career Story: Lisa, 51, HR Director

Lisa spent 22 years in an American bank and is an HR veteran. She plans to retire from the bank in 4 years' time. She said, 'I'm not intending to retire and do nothing. I'm thinking of becoming an executive coach. I heard that there is good demand for them'.

We asked her what plans she had in place to make this dream a reality and she replied, 'Nothing! It's still a long time away. I think I'll think about what I need to do in 3 years' time'.

We advised her that planning for retirement was not a one-off event. She could not expect to suddenly flick on the 'retirement switch' and expect a crowd of eager coaching clients waiting at her door.

'You need to decide what area you want to coach in and build your reputation and expertise in the next 3-4 years so you have credibility. You might need to write a book or plan to appear in a TEDTalk to position yourself as the subject matter expert. Start by getting certified and take up courses on coaching just to make sure you are sufficiently qualified in that area. All these activities take a long time to perform but would serve as the cornerstone of your brand.'

Whatever your retirement plans are, it never hurts to start thinking about how you could make them happen, today.

Step 4: Determine Your Skills Intent

The next step is to think about how to execute your Career Strategy in line with your chosen career direction and velocity.

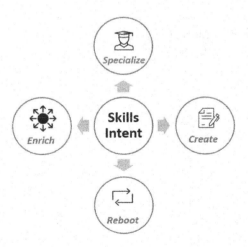

You achieve this by honing your skills to become more effective at what you intend to do, and we call this step 'determining your skills intent' and there are four ways of doing it.

Skills Specialization

As we accumulate a wealth of work experience over the years, we build a particular set of skills that we have become proficient with. These skills can be broadly categorized into 'general skills' and 'specialized skills'.

Generalists who have skills belonging to the first category have obtained broad capabilities that involve many aspects of the function or role that they do.

A good example would be from the medical field where family physicians, also known as general practitioners, are familiar with a very wide range of diseases. They have knowledge of many treatments but if patients have a rare disorder or a more serious condition, they will need to be referred to a specialist.

Specialists are doctors who have trained extensively in one domain and have very detailed knowledge of their chosen field. They are able to do a deep dive into a particular problem and find solutions or treatments for the issue. Specialists are trained along a very narrow scope and are considered subject matter experts in their field.

In the workplace, there is usually a greater demand for generalists.

A corporate executive is required to understand and manage a broad spectrum of tasks and responsibilities.

For example, HR generalists need to handle a variety of HR tasks like business partnering, compensation, hiring, performance appraisals, and talent management.

However, if asked to design a 'Compensation and Benefits' program for the company, they may not have the depth of experience to execute it and will have to consult a specialist for help.

This could lead to them being a 'jack of all trades yet master of none' which can be rather career-limiting.

One possible way of progressing your career is to specialize and concentrate on a particular focus area.

For example, HR generalists could expand their knowledge into compensation and benefits and become the subject matter expert on the latest trends and best practices, thus being able to provide even more value to their employers.

Deciding to specialize could be a good way to ensure employability and career longevity because they have now become a 'jack of all trades, master of *some*'.

Real Career Story: Adrian Choo, the Co-Author

Let me relate a personal story with you regarding specializing. In 2012, at the height of my headhunting career, I felt the urge to explore something more sustainable than executive search as LinkedIn was starting to crowd the market and would stifle headhunting in no time.

I started looking at my own skills and realize that apart from sourcing and procuring qualified candidates, one of my key areas was coaching the candidate on his Career Strategy and was exceptionally good at it.

Believing that this would be a key growth market as nobody was doing it at the time, I then decided to 'unbundle' myself and focus exclusively on this pivot and wrote a book on it which cemented me as a top career coach in Asia.

Six years later, I founded Career Agility International, focusing mainly on career resilience coaching for senior leaders.

Skills Enrichment

There are those who might have chosen to specialize very early in their careers and feel their skillsets have now grown too narrow.

For example, an accountant who spent her last 15 years in internal audit began to feel very

Enrich

nervous about her ability to pivot into another role that is outside her auditing scope. This was brought about by her company announcing that they would no longer be providing auditing services. She felt she was losing her versatility and needed to pick up wider skills and experiences to stay relevant to her employer.

We call this 'skills enrichment' because, at the core of it, the executive is broadening her areas of responsibility, enriching herself professionally, and enhancing her value to her employers. This strategy is especially useful when the individual is in a niche area that is either declining in demand or fast becoming obsolete.

For instance, an insurance salesperson who sells only life insurance policies may decide to extend her range of services to her clients and obtains the necessary training and certification to sell more complex instruments like estate and investment planning.

To engage this strategy, you can either widen the scope of your products, regions and/or responsibilities, pick up more lateral skills (e.g. coding or analytics), or move up the value chain of activities to higher value-added functions (e.g. from operational HR to strategic workforce planning).

Widening one's current domain is effective in ensuring continued employability.

Real Career Story: Reddy, 39, Logistics Manager

Reddy was a freight planning manager with a local logistics and warehousing firm. He felt it was very limiting and saw that there were many changes in the industry ahead that worried him.

For instance, he observed that companies had started outsourcing logistics to 'third-party providers' due to cost reasons and there are even 'fourth-party providers' whose job was simply to manage these third-party providers. With all these changes, he knew that if he did not do something, he would be out of a job soon.

He noticed that copious amounts of data was being generated by his logistics operations and wondered what he could do with it. He signed up for a Data Analytics Programme and learned how to build models to access and analyze the data.

With the new skills he had learnt, he managed to construct a 'load optimization model' with the information that he had and presented it to his bosses who were amazed at the cost savings it would bring! Senior management was sufficiently impressed and he got promoted.

Reddy had enlarged his skillsets by augmenting his knowledge with new technologies and tools, increasing his value to his company.

Create a Role

Besides generalists and specialists, there is a third category of executives. These are senior executives who have skills that are so unique, they find it very difficult to find a role that fits them.

Create

For instance, we have a senior client, John, whose main responsibility is to run the operations of an engineering firm. But he also managed the marketing function for the business and coached the sales teams. Additionally, he designed their client management software and led the implementation across the region. In essence, he is a uniquely talented executive who is unable to define his own role clearly.

Individuals with this profile look through job descriptions online only to realize that they are either over-qualified or under-qualified, even though they are supremely capable in their own right.

If this feels familiar, then a 'create a role' strategy would be perfect for you.

Instead of applying for existing jobs, speak to the business leaders to uncover and discuss their business challenges and how you could potentially help.

We have encountered many instances where conversations like these have led to job offers for positions that were specifically created for the particular individual.

In the case of John, he networked actively and managed to secure a meeting with the CEO of a construction firm who was so impressed with him, a special role of 'Chief of Staff' was created just for him to lead a wide variety of business improvement projects.

This strategy requires accurate targeting, good networking, effective pitching, excellent negotiating skills, and a lot of research. So, plan carefully in order to be successful and speak to your career coach if you think this complex move is the right one for you.

Reboot

Over the years, we have met quite a few executives who wished to reinvent their careers entirely.

This could entail reskilling yourself from ground zero and joining a new industry, perhaps even in an entry level position.

Reboot

It is literally a reboot of your career—a fresh start, so to speak.

For example, we recently spoke to a high-flying lawyer who has always been interested in the culinary arts and decided to set up a restaurant, selling fusion cuisine. He had to learn everything from scratch and even took up cooking classes. Today, he runs a successful chain of highly rated eateries.

If you are planning to 'reboot' your career, be prepared to learn and 'unlearn' your preconceived notions. You also need to be humble as you learn the business and be realistic in what salary you can expect.

The key strategy for 'reboot' is to stay agile in the job market and dive into new areas for career growth and longevity.

Real Life Career Story: Samuel, 45, Oil Rig Diver

Sam was a master commercial diver who spent 18 years on oil platforms at sea and earned more than US $1,000 a day for his services. He would conduct underwater repairs in the open sea, braving 3 storey high waves and dangerous currents that have swept many of his friends away.

At age 40, he realized that age was catching up with him and because of the intense physical demands of ultra-deep 'Heliox diving' (diving with a mixture of helium and oxygen), he had to prepare to exit the industry soon.

However, he did not have any non-diving skills. He realized that none of the skills he had honed over the years at sea was in demand on land. He had considered opening up a dive-shop in Phuket but the investment was too large for him. He realized he had to perform a career reboot and restart his career from ground zero.

After some research and self-examination, he rekindled his childhood passion for computer programming and at a tender age of 41, started developing commercial-grade websites for clients. He spent half a year studying web-design, UI/UX, and coding and another year apprenticing at a technology company at minimum wage just to get experience.

Today, at 49, he runs a small digital marketing agency and is very happy with the decision he took.

Step 5: Understand Your Market

Now that you have decided your career velocity, career direction, and skill intent, you need to develop a deeper understanding of your target market.

This consists of both the industry as well as the type of role that you want to be in.

By understanding the market that you wish to operate in, you will be able to be more focused and know where exactly the demand for your particular skillsets are, and hence be able to market yourself more effectively into that opportunity.

There is a classic Monty Python sketch, a British comedy show, where an accountant meets the career counsellor for the first time. The accountant mentions that he wishes to change jobs into something more exciting and adventurous and when asked what he wanted to do, declared that he wanted to be a lion tamer because it was exciting and easy to do as 'those little furry brown things' aren't too frightful. It turns out that he had mistaken anteaters for lions!

We often get candidates exhibiting similar lack of understanding of the target market which they want to join.

Some might say that they want to move into the data analytics industry as they heard it is fast growing and full of promise, but when queried about what exactly they understand about this industry, they confess, 'Not very much'.

If you do not know where the real demand is coming from or what the future trends are, you can make a wrong move and end up in a worse situation.

It would also be good for you to understand which areas of your expertise will experience increased demand.

For example, if you are an HR generalist, you may have noticed less demand for HR operations expertise due to outsourcing, and a rising demand for skills in HR analytics.

Be where the action is and pivot towards it if it aligns with your Career Strategy.

Research the industries and roles to uncover those that would require your expertise. Take note of the major companies in that sector and who the important decision makers or hiring managers are, and develop a strategy to get noticed by them.

If you do not have a full understanding of the market, find a mentor or industry expert to learn more about it.

Putting It All Together

Now that you have all this information, put it all on paper into a Career Strategy.

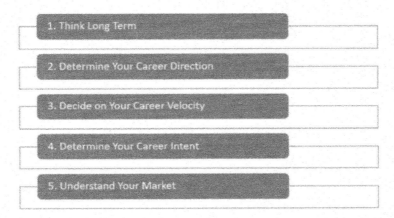

1. Think Long Term

2. Determine Your Career Direction

3. Decide on Your Career Velocity

4. Determine Your Career Intent

5. Understand Your Market

Map out the industries you want to join, the reasons why you would be good at it, and also who you can approach to learn more about this.

Commit to a plan and spend time thinking about it.

Begin networking with the key decision makers in these industries to learn more about them and also to expose yourself to their circle of influence. Let them know how you can help them and offer assistance where necessary just to get them to be aware of you.

Of course, like a craftsman's blade, you need to be consistently sharp in order to stay ahead. Keep improving yourself with the latest tools and mental models. There are many online courses you can attend—some of them are even free! Be prepared to invest money in upgrading your skills, but more importantly, be prepared to invest time, effort and discipline to learn continuously.

As you can see, crafting your Career Strategy is critical to mapping out your future career. It is a critical task that will provide the framework upon which all your career decisions will hinge. Invest time to develop one or reach out to a mentor or Career Agility coach to help you with it.

7

Career Agility

In our work, we have helped thousands of retrenched individuals land on their feet again. We noticed that they could be categorized into two distinct groups—those who managed to find a new role shortly after their exits and those who took considerably longer. Intrigued, we observed these two groups of people and discovered a fascinating difference between those who bounced back quite readily and those who didn't.

The first group possessed a basket of positive attributes that made them better prepared and more resilient to this sudden loss of employment. The second group, on the other hand, were less ready to handle this sudden turn of events, leading to a downward spiral of self-doubt and unnecessarily prolonged unemployment.

From our executive search experience, we have also met and interviewed hundreds of successful business leaders who have come a long way in their careers and would be regarded by many as successful and at the top of their game. When we asked them what they felt were the traits that enabled them to succeed in their careers, they shared that it was a matter of having a set of habits, mindsets, and practices. This empowered them to act upon opportunities and avoid impending threats, even unforeseen ones.

Upon further research, we successfully identified these attributes that were the key enablers behind their career success and decided to name this trait 'Career Agility'.

In other words, individuals with a high degree of Career Agility achieved their career goals more easily and in a shorter time. They not only survived better in whatever role they were in, but they *thrived*.

Being career agile can help you get promoted if you are a career accelerator, avoid retrenchment if you seek job security, identify new and exciting roles if you are an opportunity seeker, and even land a job quickly if you are an urgent job hunter.

However, one of the most exciting findings was that Career Agility was a set of skills that can be learnt by anyone.

To our dismay, we see many busy executives who are too weighed down by the daily grind of work activities and the pursuit of KPIs (Key Performance Indicators) to realize that they need to learn how to improve their Career Agility, and so, end up missing out on opportunities along their way.

Real Career Stories: Lincoln, 44

Everybody knew Lincoln would be a highflyer from the very first day he started work at a major oil company. Graduating with a First-class Honours from a top British University, he had also been the president of their student body and was also a star sportsman.

Peers nicknamed him 'Gold dust' and everyone watched his career very closely when he first joined the company after graduating.

He started out as their sales executive and was quickly promoted to manager. He realized that the manufacturing sector he was covering was a declining one and sought permission to grow and develop the faster-growing bio-medical one, where he achieved phenomenal sales growth, catching the attention of the Asia CEO who took him under his wing and promoted him again.

In 2003, he foresaw the rise of online shopping and started his company's first online store that made them the market leader in the space. He then mastered the art of digital marketing and he networked his way into Amazon, his vendors' circles, and was soon hired by them to be their regional director.

Lincoln's career had been a series of well-planned and excellently executed moves, each one more deliberately planned than the previous. He had the foresight to seize on new growth markets and reinvent himself repeatedly. He knew how to leverage the power of networks to get noticed and was brought onboard new and faster growing companies. Lincoln was career agile and his career was roaring away.

What is Career Agility?

'Career Agility is the ability to anticipate and respond appropriately to career opportunity and threats, to achieve career longevity and satisfaction.'

It means that being career agile entails a certain degree of versatility, adaptability, and proactiveness in terms of managing your own career. It means being able to balance on a tightrope and respond quickly and deliberately to changes in the environment.

But what are the key variables that one needs to react to? To have a better understanding of that, we need to go back to the basics.

Staying Employed is Economics 101

Back in school, we learnt in Economics 101 that almost everything boils down to supply and demand.

Staying employed is no different. It is merely a matter of supply and demand of skills in the skills market. In recent years, this skills market has become global with a free flow of talents physically crossing borders to work anywhere.

Furthermore, the pandemic has been a game-changer in terms of skills mobility because the distance economy allowed employees to work from home, hence employees need not even be in-country to do the job.

As a result, companies are now benefiting from the wide availability of skills at varying levels of competency and prices, irrespective of geographic location.

For instance, someone managing a virtual customer support centre need not be based in the country where the calls are coming from. For example, a US company based in Singapore managing Asia Pacific could have the call-centre team in Manila, and the team manager could be based in Bangkok.

Therefore, the skills market has truly gone global and has become far more complicated than ever.

For better understanding, let us examine the 2 key elements involved—skills demand and skills supply.

Understanding and Anticipating Demand for Skills

When you choose a surgeon to perform a delicate operation, do you select him/her based on his looks, birth month, star-sign, or do you select them based on their experience in handling your condition and their proven ability to treat it?

Chances are, you are selecting them based on their skills.

This logic extends beyond just engaging medical practitioners. It also applies to any job. For example, if you are looking for a plumber to fix a choked sink, you would want someone who is qualified and has the right skills and experience to get the job done and probably would not mind paying more for one who could do it quicker and better.

This is what 'skills demand' looks like. When the user, customer, or employer has a problem that can be best solved by someone with a particular set of skills and expertise, they are willing to pay for it and hence demand is created.

The big question to ask then is, 'Do you know where the skills demand is coming from?'

To understand skills demand, we need to conduct an industry analysis and a role analysis.

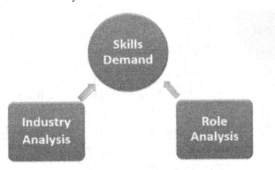

• *Industry Analysis*

Take an in-depth look at your own industry, or the industry you wish to target. Is it growing or shrinking? The answer to this can be clear for some industries, for example, newspaper printing is in decline as users prefer to consume their news online.

For others, the sector could be growing unevenly, offering both opportunities and threats at the same time.

Take the logistics industry where demand for international deliveries via sea freight may be declining as the price of airfreight comes down, but at the same time, last mile delivery companies have seen phenomenal growth during the Covid-19 pandemic when everyone was shopping from home. Are these trends here to stay?

Study the trends closely and ask the following questions:

Which part of my industry or target industry is:

- Growing in demand and how can I become a part of it?
- Heading towards obsolescence and how can I pivot out of it?
- Being disrupted and how I can be part of that disruptive technology?
- Moving to cheaper locations and how can I avoid being retrenched?
- Being replaced by newer technologies or AI and how can I upskill for it?
- Being reinvented and how can I get into it?

Real Life Career Story: Bryan, 45, Cloud Expert

Bryan always prided himself as a 'technology geek', teaching himself how to program in C+ at an early age. He started his career in IBM as a systems engineer, handling his clients' server-farms throughout the late 1990s.

One day, on a family vacation to the US, he came across an article touting how 'cloud' technology was going to be the next big thing. He had not heard of that and it sparked his curiosity.

Bryan then conducted research into this space and realized that a large part of what he did was ready for disruption and decided to move into this space.

'Oh, it's just another fad.' Many people laughed at him when he shared this idea with them in 2004, but he persevered and joined a new division of on online shopping portal which was looking at going into this space in a big way.

Years later, Bryan became a senior technologist at this company, Amazon Web Services, that grew into one of the largest cloud services providers in the world and today, is a much sought after expert.

'Had I not analyzed my industry and made a conscious effort to pivot into a high growth area, I would still be walking around in server-farms and would have probably died of boredom by now, or be worried about my career longevity. However, looking ahead and looking around the bend helped me to stay fresh and be in demand.'

One way to begin identifying important trends is to conduct market research. Researching industries is not difficult, even though many have reported that they do not know where to start because there is just too much information out there.

- Start with corporate websites. Look at your own company's website to read about your leadership team's point of view on the future of your industry. How is the market changing and where is it heading? You might even want to research your competitors' websites to get their point of view on the market as well. Are there areas they are investing heavily in? Gather all that information into a notebook.

- Map all the business partners, suppliers, vendors, distributors, and customers that form the ecosystem of the industry you are researching. Which of these are growing and which aren't? Build a larger picture of what each of these organizations focus on, connecting the dots on the unique relationships within the industry. Expand the information now to include contacts you know in the market who work at or have conducted business with some of these organizations.

- Watch for interesting announcements. Look for significant events—new alliances, partnerships or joint ventures. Are there any new products or new markets? Have there been products that have been shelved or companies that have exited the market? What do these events mean to the industry equilibrium? Does a particular new player to the market mean a decline in the market leader's position? Is this a trend or a permanent disruption?

  For example, if you are an expert in regional tax laws and read an announcement that a private equity firm was acquiring a start-up with ground breaking AI bots that could automate taxation processes, you could directly approach the investing firm to see if they needed anyone with the legal knowledge needed to power that new AI engine.

- Compile all the information gathered from your research and speak to the people in the industry to get their own points of view regarding growth areas. You can leverage LinkedIn as a powerful enabler in this regard by reaching out to the key people in those markets and connecting with them.

- Besides finding out what the experts think about the future of their own industries, you might want to form your own predictions regarding the industry. Where do you think the market is heading in 10 years' time? What are the trends and even 'micro-trends' that could lead to 'the next big thing'? Develop your own point of view and vision, and work towards being a part of that change or be the disruption!

- **Role Analysis**

To fully understand skills demand, apart from researching the industry, further fact-finding is needed on the nature of work required.

This is even more important as roles evolve quickly these days and the skills needed for these roles also keep changing.

For instance, schoolteachers used to only have to stand up and teach their students the 3 Rs of education. Today, they need emotional-coaching skills, parent-management skills as well as be technologically proficient enough to create content, upload it, and manage the learning management platforms the schools are on.

It is important to realize that depending on the role, specific skills are required.

However, listing your skills may not always be easy because they can be difficult to articulate, let alone identify.

For instance, is managing a 12-person sales team a skill? How about managing a $200 million business? How would you describe that ability?

Skills can also be deceivingly complex and multi-layered. If you asked a sales manager what his key skill was, he would probably reply, 'Selling things'.

However, if you drilled deep enough, you would see that to be a truly effective and successful sales leader, he would need the plethora of skills listed below:

• *Account management*	• *Marketing strategy*
• *Team management*	• *Funnel management*
• *Pipeline management*	• *Sales operations*
• *Sales training*	• *Sales forecasting*
• *Coaching*	• *Price modelling*
• *Negotiations*	• *Sales data analysis*
• *Stakeholder management*	• *Networking*
• *Client relationship management (CRM)*	• *Consumer understanding*
• *Software management*	• *Digital marketing*

Sometimes, not all these skills are in demand at the same time by the same organization, and could be outsourced (e.g. CRM software management) whereas others could be growing in demand at exponential rates (e.g. digital marketing).

So, it is important to know how roles are evolving and what skills are needed.

Understanding and Articulating the Supply of Skills

There is an old story told about a ship owner who had problems with his engine that nobody could repair. He decided to engage an old engineer to have a look and see if he could fix it. The engineer took one glance at the machine, took out his wrench, and gave 3 hard knocks on the back of one of the valves. To everyone's surprise, the engine came back to life and was working perfectly again.

He presented an invoice of $5,000 to the ship owner for repairs and the ship owner baulked at the amount! 'It took you only five seconds and three knocks! I'm not paying for $5,000 for that!'

The old engineer agreed, tore the invoice up, and submitted a new one which read:

Item #1: Five seconds and three knocks	$1.00
Item #2: Knowing where to knock and how hard to knock	$4,999.00

We all get paid for the valuable services we provide. In our career, we are being hired by our organization for the skills that we bring to work on a daily basis. We create value for our clients, colleagues, and ultimately, to our employer and that is what we get paid for. In fact, it has been said that the salary we get is actually the company's monthly subscription to our skills and contribution.

 The supply of skills is what you have to offer the employment market!

It is the 'currency' you use to exchange with your employers for your salary.

As far as being able to provide the skills to meet the demand goes, you need to ask yourself the following questions and answer them honestly.

1. Can you articulate and list your repertoire of skills?
2. Are your skills still relevant in today's market?
3. Will your skills be relevant for tomorrow's market?
4. How proficient are you at these skills?
5. Are your skills industry-specific or are they transferable to another industry?
6. Which other industries would love to buy your skills?

7. What are the future skills needed by the market, and how would you acquire them?
8. What are the gaps in your skills and how would you close them?

To meet the market demand for current and future skills, you need to conduct a 'skills audit' and determine your strengths as well as your areas of development.

We must regularly update our set of skills to ensure that they are continually in demand in the market. Even if you are already happily employed by your company, we need to consistently look at ways to increase our value to our organization.

But how do we do it?

Simple.

We do it by enhancing our skills. There are 3 basic ways to do that: up-skill, cross-skill, and deep- skill.

Up-skill

We may be experts in most of what we do, but there are always new things to learn. Observe what your bosses can do that you aren't ready to handle.

For instance, maybe she handles the board of directors very well, or is able to engage C-suite clients easily. Learn how she does it by either asking her for advice, or just through observation. Identify the skills and learn from them.

Cross-skill

What can your colleagues do that you can't? If you are in supply-chain, how about learning how finance calculates and monitors the cost of inventory, or how IT uses their enterprise software to manage the optimization of stock levels.

Learn and master new skills from other functions as this will make you more valuable to the organization. During times of downsizing, being 'cross-skilled' makes you less likely to be retrenched.

Deep-skill

Be a master at whatever you are doing. Nurture your skills in your chosen profession to be the subject matter expert. Be the 'go-to person' whom everyone thinks of consulting whenever they face a problem. You can pick up new skills through investing in formal training or even signing up for free online courses.

Today, it is no longer a 'job market' but a 'skills market', and you should always look for ways to improve yourself. Recognize that skills have expiry dates and there are always cheaper, faster, and better-skilled people waiting to take your job.

Keep improving your skills repertoire!

What Career Agility is Really about

To sum it up, being career agile is all about understanding where the demand for skills is and knowing how you can supply these skills to the market. It's about staying at the intersection of both curves and remaining there despite changes to the employment market. It's all about being adaptable and staying employable.

Part D

Adapting to the New Model

8

Introducing the Career Animals Model

In the previous section, we learnt how to achieve career longevity and career satisfaction via sound strategies and went into great detail about what Career Agility means. In this chapter, we will discuss how to apply the Career Agility Model in the real world.

To illustrate this better, we created a matrix model that is both practical and easy to understand, called the Career Animals Model.

A Quick Recap

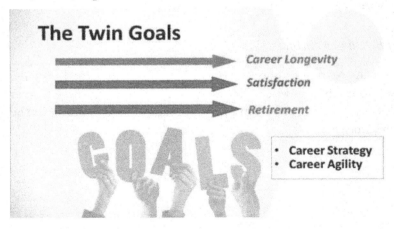

In order to achieve sustainable career success, we have identified the two key factors that will help attain that goal. These are:

A. Career Strategy

Recall that in Chapter 5, Career Strategy is defined as *'a plan you develop based on self-knowledge and market trends, identifying your strengths, weaknesses, passion, and values as well as various market opportunities and threats looming over your horizon'*. It is the masterplan you create that will chart the future of your career and act as the roadmap which you will use as a guide for determining your career moves.

B. Career Agility

In Chapter 7, we defined Career Agility as *'the ability to anticipate and respond appropriately to career opportunities and threats to achieve career longevity and satisfaction'*. It is all about how prepared and capable you are in the face of an evolving world of work. This will enable you to seize opportunities and avoid pitfalls that may present themselves in your career in the future.

The Career Animals Model

In constructing a model that can be easily understood visually, we took these two attributes of Career Strategy and Career Agility and mapped them on two separate axes, resulting in the chart below.

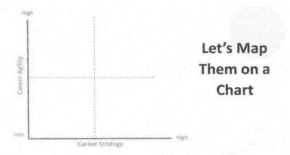

This results in four different zones representing the four combinations of Career Agility/Career Strategy areas on the chart, partitioning the profiles into different quadrants. The four profiles then clearly show up as follows:

Each of these profiles in their respective quadrants have their own shared attributes and, from our research, we were able to extract these attributes and make recommendations based on them.

To further simplify this 4-Quadrant model, we decided to attach animal avatars to them: Career Lion, Career Canary, Career T-Rex, And Career Panda.

This can be represented more clearly in the diagram below:

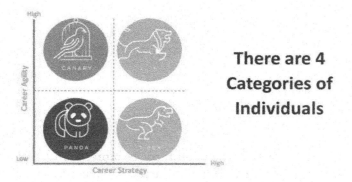

Individuals who possess different degrees of Career Agility and Career Strategy now fall into these four broad categories and career enhancing recommendations can now be created for them.

Some Caveats regarding the Career Animals Model

Before we proceed, we would like to categorically state the following caveats regarding the use of our Career Animals Model.

These animal avatars are simply metaphorical representations of individual profiles corresponding to each quadrant.

These four animals are *not* labels attached to individuals and hence do not have any inherently 'good' or 'bad' connotations about their personal character or performance at work and we recommend that users of this model likewise refrain from labelling themselves or others with these animal names.

We also want to highlight that the profiles are not permanent but are a momentary snapshot of their attributes at a single point in time. In fact, our data has shown that with the right training and coaching in Career Strategy and Career Agility, in as little as 3 months, individuals have shown marked improvement in their scores.

Finally, we wish to reiterate that this Career Animals Model was created only as a guide and serves not to judge but to be a starting point for you to begin thinking about your career and how to improve it. Unlike blood pressure measurements or cholesterol level tests, the scores are not absolute and will vary from one person to another, hence it would be unfair to make direct comparisons regarding who has a better career.

Welcome to the Jungle: Introducing the Career Animals

- **The Career Lions** are both high in Career Agility and Career Strategy.
- **The Career Canaries** are high in Career Agility but do not have a strong Career Strategy yet.
- **The Career T-Rexes** have a well-developed Career Strategy but need to improve their Career Agility.
- And finally, there are **the Career Pandas** who do not have a strong working Career Strategy yet and have not been developing their Career Agility in recent times.

We shall now analyze each avatar in greater detail.

The Career Lion

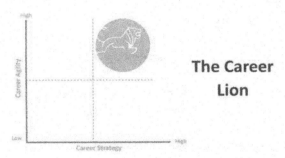

Profiles that are represented in this quadrant display high levels of Career Agility and Career Strategy. They have well thought-out career plans and have kept an eye on their career trajectory over the years.

They are often up to date with their skills and exhibit a good understanding of where their profession or industry is headed and are proactively navigating their careers towards high growth areas or away from sunset industries.

Because of their high skills level and relevance to the market, they are often sought after by other departments or even by other companies outside their industry because of their reputation and highly transferable skills and capabilities.

An example of a Career Lion would be Elon Musk, the visionary technologist and founder of Tesla, SpaceX, and the Boring Company. Each of these companies, when founded, fulfilled a future need that did not exist at that time. He was able to see beyond the present market needs and built up his capabilities in anticipation of it. As a result, he has managed to stay relevant and thrive in a disruptive and fast-changing environment.

Real Career Story: Tommy, HR SVP, 42,
The Career Lion

After graduation, Tommy started out as a product engineer with a US-based telecommunications company in the 1990s. Early in his career, he would design hardware solutions for 'cutting edge' technology products like modems and pagers, but by the early 2000s, he realized that these products would soon be obsolete.

He also realized that as a product engineer based in the UK, his career would plateau quickly, and probably stop progressing beyond the product manager level. Getting any higher up the hierarchy would be challenging, especially given that the global centre of product development was in the US.

As a result, he took the bold step of volunteering for several 'HR Change Management' projects in his business unit and picked up certain HR skills. After 18 months, he felt ready to make a career switch and pivoted into a full-time HR role in another company, even though he had to take a slightly lower salary.

He persevered in his newly adopted field and evolved into a very capable HR leader with a strong background in the technology sector. Today, he is a senior vice president of HR with a global software company and is one of the most respected voices in the industry.

Although the Career Lion, like an actual lion, is always on the prowl for better opportunities within their companies or industries, they can sometimes get complacent with their position and become too comfortable on their lofty perch. As such, they need to consider how to stay ahead of the game.

Career Lions need to maintain their edge at all times because there are always other Career Lions lurking around, hunting in their domain as well. Some of these competitors could take the form of younger, hungrier lions waiting to seize a piece of your prize.

If you are a Career Lion, you should keep your eye out for new opportunities ahead of your rivals and broaden your horizons to accommodate other fields. This could take the form of adjacent industries or adjacent skillsets that could act as new 'hunting grounds', like Tommy in our career story pivoting into an entirely new domain when the old lands became dry.

Career Lions also need to find ways to continuously hone their Career Agility, keeping a look out for new trends that could disrupt their careers, or better still, trends that could grow into huge untapped opportunities in the future. One good way of trendspotting would be to network widely with other Career Lions within the industry and make connections and inroads into previously unexplored territories.

The Career Canary

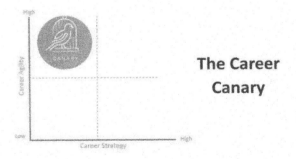

Profiles that fall into this quadrant are described as being capable but have possibly been in their comfort zones for a bit too long. Many have been in the same company or role for long periods of time and may have lost their edge in the external talent market.

Like real canaries, they have lived comfortably in the safety of their cages for many years and tend to view it as a shield keeping predators out rather than an enclosure keeping them in. They treasure the security that a stable environment provides and even when given a chance to fly away, might choose to shut the door of the cage and stay put. Some may have even forgotten how to fly!

Career Canaries often display high levels of Career Agility, but for various personal or professional reasons, do not have a fully fleshed-out Career Strategy.

A possible reason for this could be complacency as they have been in their roles, industries, or even under the wings of specific leaders for so long that they have never really had to think about their futures, assuming status quo was the order of the day; or perhaps, they never needed to have a Career Strategy at all because their employers had been taking care of their career all this while.

Real Career Story: Lisa, Fuels Blending Operations Manager, 46, The Career Canary

Lisa spent the past 25 years of her career with a large oil and gas company. She joined as a management trainee and was immediately identified as a high potential executive and was fast-tracked through the system, taking on increasingly challenging roles that gave her deeper exposure to the company and the oil industry.

Feeling secure in her role, she had been approached many times by potential employers—competitors as well as technology companies—who saw value in her experience, skills, and leadership when she was in her late 30s and early 40s. She declined speaking with any of them, rebuffing them with statements like 'Don't call me again because I'm very happy here. I'm going to retire in this company'.

Last year, her company was acquired by a private equity firm and she was transferred to a much smaller role under a tyrannical boss who made life very difficult for her. In frustration, she resigned and has been facing difficulty landing a similar role because the oil and gas industry has seen negative growth, and her skillsets were too specialized to be applied elsewhere. She is currently unemployed and considers herself 'unemployable'.

Career Canaries are usually good contributors to their business and are effective at navigating their internal organization. However, as mentioned earlier, they often place too much trust in their company for career development and direction. Whilst this might have worked for them before, in today's complex and uncertain environment where economic pressures exert untold stress on corporations, it would be risky to assume that the halcyon days will continue indefinitely.

Their much-venerated sponsor could retire, leaving them out in the cold, or the company might decide to terminate their entire business division. When changes happen, the Career Canary could face some unpleasant realities such as an undesired change in job scope or even retrenchment.

If you identify as a Career Canary, maintaining the status quo is risky and there is imminent danger of losing your own relevance to the external skills market. It is time to wrest control of your career back into your own hands. The first step to improving your situation is to recognize that you could actually be a Career Canary. One simple question to make that determination is to ask yourself this difficult question, 'What would happen if I get retrenched tomorrow?'

Do you have a Plan B? Do you know of another division or external company who would love to have you on their team? More importantly, do they know of you? Are you aware of any skills gaps that might prevent you from qualifying for that job?

If you have no contingencies in place, you could be at risk of being unemployed for a period of time should your role be made redundant due to corporate restructuring.

There also needs to be an internal mindset shift towards overcoming the fear of the unknown. Many Career Canaries stay with the same organization because of this. Conducting more research to find more information or insights will help them make better decisions.

Realize that the safe environment that protects you from the external world is actually caging you in. Start looking for the exits and strengthen your wings for flight. Take charge of your Career Strategy and start building a robust plan for a future outside of your current environment.

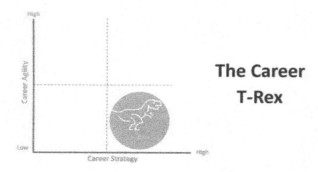

The Career T-Rex

The profiles that conform to the lower right quadrant are usually the ones who seem to have everything planned but are unable to break out of their career plateau or glass ceiling. Even though their Career Strategy seems well thought-out, they are unable to secure that much-desired promotion internally or to land their dream job externally. As a result, they feel helpless and frustrated, much like the fearsome T-Rex, perceived as the king of all dinosaurs with its fierce look and huge size, but their undersized arms indicating limited hunting ability.

The Career T-Rex may face a glass ceiling due to his/her lack of relevant experience and poor mastery of important skills.

Real Career Story: Richard, 52, IT Manager, The Career T-Rex

It was Richard's third attempt at getting promoted but he was once again denied. The role went to a younger executive who, he felt, had less experience, talent, and capability.

'The organization is biased against me,' he whispered to himself. 'Never mind, I'll wait for the next promotion cycle.'

Richard had spent 15 years with the bank where he worked and was heading a small IT department in charge of the legacy solutions business. This unit maintained the backup mainframe servers and played a highly specialized role.

He was technically highly skilled in these outdated systems but never had the time nor inclination to update his knowledge to more modern cloud-based technologies.

He had planned to be an IT Director since he was 35 and had applied for countless senior leadership roles but had always been rejected and he was feeling frustrated. The truth was that potential employers viewed him as 'the legacy guy' and simply doubted his ability to adapt to new technologies.

'I'm certain someday, somebody will recognize my talent and my recently earned MBA and offer me the IT Director job.'

If you identify as a *Career T-Rex*, one of the first things you need to do is to realize that you might have gaps in your Career Agility.

Ask yourself

- Are you sufficiently skilled in the areas that are in demand?
- Is your reputation in the company or the industry helping or hurting your chances at acceleration?
- Are you positioned correctly for the role you want and are you interviewing strategically for them?

Even though you might think that you have a good working Career Strategy, it may not be the right one for you at this point in your career or it can even be flawed. Check your assumptions and get objective insight from either your mentor or your career coach.

If you have not had any luck landing external roles or are bypassed for internal promotions, reflect on what might be missing in your profile. Review your level of Career Agility again and upgrade your skills as necessary.

The Career Panda

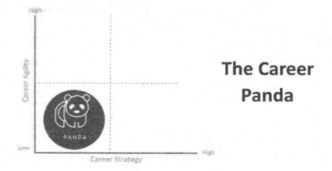

The lower left quadrant represents profiles displaying lower proficiency in both Career Strategy and Career Agility. They do not have any functioning career plans beyond turning up for work in the morning and going home to the family in the evenings. Steadfast and structured, they are often good at what they do, probably because they have been doing the same tasks for many years and shun any possibility of taking on any new roles.

Should a change in business model or a re-organization happen, they will be the first to protest and may even refuse to adapt to the new requirements. Because they have been in their comfort zone for many years, they are not the most adaptable and may be inclined to resist change, much like the pandas in the wild who live within very narrow parameters. Surviving in only one climate and eating only one type of bamboo, pandas are highly endangered and could face extinction should an environmental shift happen.

Like their cuddly and cute counterparts, Career Pandas prefer to remain in their comfort zone and not experience any change at all. Trusting their futures entirely to their employers, they neither worry nor fret over the externalities of the business, having full faith that the company will look after them come rain or sunshine. Their skills may not be up to date as they have might have been doing the same repetitive work for many years and never bothered to upgrade themselves because they do not see the need to do so.

Real Career Story: May, 49, Project Manager, The Career Panda

Retrenched at 45, May spent 20 years in her company, a telecommunications service provider. She had graduated with a degree in computer engineering from a prestigious university and was considered one of her company's top talent when she joined. She was quickly adopted by a high-ranking sponsor who made sure she never had to bid for the most exciting projects and had been given any role she desired. She was enviously considered the protégé of that senior leader.

In 2012, her sponsor was fired for some impropriety and, suddenly, May was left defenceless and tarred by her sponsor's negative reputation. Nobody wanted to give her any good projects to manage and the economic slump of 2015 did not help either as project pipelines dried up.

The CEO was a close friend so he did not fire her even though she was not contributing much to the business.

Instead of upgrading her skills or finding a new sponsor, she just lingered on and tried to make herself useful with any small projects she could find, including managing the pantry and organizing ad-hoc outings and corporate events like the Annual Dinner and Dance. Once, she even took over as the Receptionist for four months when her colleague went on maternity leave.

For five years, she floated from role to role, never really delving into the IT projects that came and went. 'After all, I wasn't too worried because my friend, the CEO, won't fire me.' She confessed. Meanwhile, she had lost touch with the latest software changes and had lost her edge and relevance to the market.

In 2017, the CEO retired and she was retrenched. At age 45, she sought an IT project manager role in another telco with a similar salary. She was called up for several job interviews because her profile looked good on paper, but when queried on her skills and latest projects, she could not cite any examples that weren't 6 years old. She was once asked, 'What is your greatest skill?' and she replied honestly, 'I used to manage complex multi-region solutions, but today, I'm really good at knitting sweaters as it's my hobby.'

Needless to say, she never found another corporate job and has been driving for Uber 'temporarily until the right job comes along' since her retrenchment 4 years ago.

If you identify as a Career Panda, you will need to come to terms with the fact that you may have been in your comfort zone for too long and are highly vulnerable to any sudden change in the corporate environment. You could possibly be one disruptive new technology, one cost-savings exercise, or one new boss away from being unemployable.

The truth is that because of skills irrelevance, Career Pandas are often the first to be retrenched. They need to work on both their Career Strategy and Career Agility urgently to retain their career longevity. If you are a Career Panda, begin with an honest skills audit. List as many of your skills that you can think of and ask yourself the following questions:

My Skills Audit

- How many skills do I have?
- Are they updated and relevant?
- Is there good demand for these skills?
- Are they so specialized that they are not transferable to another industry?
- Can an RPA (Robotic Software Automation) do it?
- Can someone younger, cheaper, or located offshore do it?

If the answers are beginning to make you nervous, it is time to make another list.

My Skills Gaps

- What are the skills in demand today and will be in demand in the next 5 years?
- Would I enjoy acquiring and performing those skills?
- Are those skills in line with my Career Strategy?
- Would my previous or current skills complement this list of skills?
- How would I go about acquiring those new skills?

Identify your skills gaps and take action. Sign up for courses and take every chance to work on projects that require them, even if it means extra work hours or apprehension about the daunting task ahead.

You also need to think long-term. Take a hard look at your Career Strategy and see where you plan to be in 5 years' time and whether it is realistic. Do you have a clear pathway to that goal? Are you well networked into that target industry or dream job? Start making a plan and take action because the volatile business environment does not give us the luxury of time to sit around and react only when changes happen.

Using the Career Animals Model

We reiterate that this model only serves as a guide and was never designed to pigeonhole or label any particular individual.

You may find yourself relating to one or a combination of the Career Animals, but whichever avatar you identify with, the career advice that was shared in this chapter holds true to most of us at some baseline level.

To find out what Career Animal you are, you can try the career quiz (https://quiz.CareerAgility.org) and you will receive a detailed basic report which includes some advice on how to navigate your career.

The diagnosis is a snapshot of this moment in your career journey and your current frame of mind. Do not fret if the results are not ideal as there is no right or wrong. Trying the career quiz multiple times to achieve better results defeats its purpose.

Your career quiz results can be a good starting point for you to have conversations with your mentors, supervisors, leaders, and peers. Based on these conversations, you can now create a long-term Career Strategy and some short-term career goals to drive your career in the direction you want.

 Scan this QR Code or visit https://quiz. CareerAgility.org to find out what Career Animal you are! Use the Promotional code PARADOXBOOK to enjoy 50% off the Full Report!

Part E

Applying the New Model

9

Self-Assessment

'If you know the enemy and know yourself, you need not fear the result of a hundred battles. If you know yourself but not the enemy, for every victory gained, you will also suffer a defeat. If you know neither the enemy nor yourself, you will succumb in every battle.'

—*Sun Tzu*

Knowing yourself is critical in the development of your Career Strategy for two reasons.

Firstly, in order to chart your own destiny, you will need to know what you want and more importantly, what you don't want. A map without a destination is just a piece of paper with scribbled lines and pictures. Secondly, self-awareness allows you to understand who and what you are, what you can offer, and the places that would love to have your skills, expertise, and knowledge.

Remember that you are selling a product which is YOU and like all effective salespeople, you need to know what you're selling. Without this understanding of yourself and what you have to offer, few people would 'buy' you.

In this chapter, we will delve deeper into each self-discovery component—skills, wants, interests, values, limitations, and personality. We will discuss how to articulate them, the implications of each of these variables and, finally, put everything into a coherent picture.

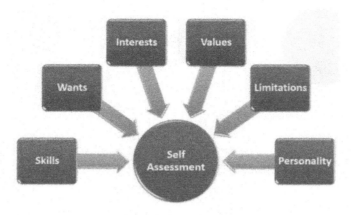

What are Your Skills?

We have previously discussed the importance of skills in Career Agility. To be resilient in your career, your skills have to be constantly sharpened, deepened, and updated. We also discussed cross-skilling and upskilling which involves learning from your peers as well as your leaders.

In this section, we will go into greater detail how to articulate your skills concisely and accurately.

One question we ask our clients is, 'What is your superpower?'

We also ask them, 'Do you know what sets you apart from your peers? What are you great at that others cannot do as well?'

In response, we often hear a list of key words like 'I'm good at project management, business development, leadership, communications' or other generic responses. At face value, they sound pretty good. But these words alone are insufficient in describing your actual capabilities and your audience will probably be thinking, 'Project Management? That's nice, but project managing what? How big was the project? How much was the budget? How long did it take to complete? Who were the people you worked with? How did this project help the organization?'

Simply using generic descriptions like these lack scale, scope, and context, leaving the listener curious and uninformed. Where possible, always provide the context when articulating your skills.

Did you run a marketing project or a technology upgrade project, or a team-bonding event?

So when asked, 'What is your superpower?', you might answer, 'I have successfully project managed large-scale regional supply chain systems implementations in the F&B and medical industries,' or 'I am very experienced in supply chain projects, focusing mostly on large enterprise-wide upgrades and operational effectiveness for clients in F&B and medical industries'.

Real Life Career Story: Thomas, 36, Insurance Sales Executive

Thomas had been an insurance salesman all his career. He started in this industry fresh out of university and found that he actually enjoyed the freedom and independence that selling personal insurance brought. The money was quite reasonable too and he was able to afford his annual European ski holiday which he was quite thankful for.

One drawback, however, was when he was asked what he did for a living. At parties, he would get shifty glances whenever he replied, 'I sell insurance,' and many people would avoid him, fearing that he would be the stereotypical pesky insurance salesman trying to get a deal out of them.

One day, his 5-year-old daughter asked him, 'My friend Cynthia's daddy is a doctor. What do you do, Daddy?'.

Thomas paused and thought, 'How would I explain my job to my daughter in simple enough terms that she can understand?'

He then replied, 'Daddy helps people to prepare themselves before something bad happens, so that they don't have to worry about it'.

He realized that this was actually his superpower, and from then on, he would introduce himself at parties as, 'I help people prepare themselves financially so they can have peace of mind to do the things they love'. He has been receiving more positive responses at parties since.

There are many ways to position your superpower and skill, but it's important to give it context and scope. Do not rely on oversimplified key words and hope the listener will fill in the blanks with their own imagination.

 Here is an exercise:
List your top 10 latest skills. In fact, these are the very skills you are being paid for in your current job. Next to each skill, write down the scope, scale, industry, clients, budget size, number of people involved, and other relevant information.

This may be difficult, even tedious, but it is well worth the effort.

My Superpower Exercise:

Top Skill	Scale	Industry	Clients	Scope	Size	Results
Selling	Asia Region	Medical Devices	Major Hospitals	Surgical Instruments	$58 million	Annual Growth of 12%
Team Leadership	Team of 92 people	Real Estate	Commercial clients	Talent acquisition and training	$1.4 billion	84% closing success rate

In the first example above, the Individual's superpower is driving 12% year-on-year sales of a $58 million Asia-Pacific portfolio of surgical instruments, selling to major hospitals in the region.

Skills You Enjoy vs Skills You Dislike

Review your list again and look at which skills you enjoy.

It is important to also identify which skills bring you meaning and satisfaction and which ones lead to you feeling burnt-out.

For instance, a manager might find 'counselling' to be interesting and emotionally rewarding but having to counsel 15 of his staff every week might prove too draining for him/her.

Look for roles with skill requirements that you will be utilizing frequently. Seek jobs that emphasize these criteria and pursue these roles aggressively.

You could also review all your previous roles or jobs to uncover skills you enjoyed and also those you didn't. What were you doing that made the work so enjoyable? List these skills and look for them in your next role.

What do you really want (and don't want) to do?

Steve Jobs famously said, 'The only way to do great work is to love what you do'.

Having clarity around what you want *more* and *less of* is important in determining the type of role that can keep you satisfied and happy. When you were starting out in your career, you may have been drawn to your profession because you enjoyed the environment or the tasks. Many chose vocations based on their best subjects at school or tried multiple temporary jobs before settling on one that seemed right for them. As a mid-career executive, however, knowing the nature of the role you want will help identify your dream job so that you will be prepared when the right one comes along.

To know what the ideal job looks like, try this exercise.

Want More of	Want Less of
• Larger regional responsibility • Manage a larger team • Handle 2 new divisions • Bigger Salary • More autonomy	• Micro-managing boss • Political or toxic environment • Operational role—wants to be involved in strategic planning • Weekend work

What I want More/Less of

Once you have identified what you really want and what you don't want, you will have a better picture of whether to progress or reject whatever opportunity comes before you.

Real Career Stories: Caroline, 41, Legal Eagle

Caroline was the top litigator in her law firm. She was one of the top billers and made a lot of money. However, the long hours of standing in court and busy schedules started to give her a bad back and it only got worse as her career progressed.

'I know the money is great, but I also realize that there is only so much damage my body can take before I break down.'

So, she made a bold move and took a sabbatical which lasted one year, just to give her back time to recover and heal.

During that year-long break, she took up yoga and became a certified instructor.

Once her back was back to normal again, she took up a lecturing position at a training institute with a less punishing schedule.

Pursuing Your Interests

Many people follow their heart and gravitate towards roles or industries based on their interests. For example, you might have a keen interest in health and nutrition and keeping fit. But, at the same time, you also have an interest in numbers and having done some research and several internships, you realize that you're very suited to the healthcare industry. Consequently, you could effectively choose a finance vocation in a hospital or a large pharmaceutical MNC.

If you are at a career crossroad, it might be a good idea to take a few steps back and analyze where your interests lie. What aspects of your previous roles were the most enjoyable and meaningful to you?

One retired army officer was very passionate about golf. After retiring, he would spend most afternoons on the greens perfecting his chosen sport. After some months, he decided to start a company organizing golfing trips overseas as well as trading in golfing equipment. He decided that his next role would be passion-led, and never looked back. He said, 'When you are doing what you are most passionate about, it isn't work!'

Indeed, if you are fortunate enough to be in a job or an industry you are really passionate about, you are probably enjoying every moment of it. If you aren't already energized by your current job, switching to an industry you are interested in could re-energize your career and bring more meaning to your life.

Many clients we work with are unable to express their interests. Most stumble through career choices based on what they know or what they felt they were good at, not realizing that what they are good at may not be what they enjoy the most and could cause burn-out in the long run.

Many clients chose their careers based on earning potential. They were quick to take up better-paying jobs but eventually realized that jobs with higher salaries often came at a correspondingly high personal cost. They often had to sacrifice something of value like time with their family, stress-free living, and possibly even their health. Some people who have chosen their careers based on earning potential alone have ended up in professions that they disliked but were unable to leave because they had grown too accustomed to the money.

Real Life Career Story: Serene, Baker

Serene worked in HR for many years. Her specialization was in recruitment and she successfully recruited individuals for her organization, a technology giant, for about 8 years.

She then joined a headhunting agency because the commissions were attractive. She was doing well, but was feeling increasingly conflicted as her toddlers started pre-school and eventually primary school.

She always had an interest in baking and would involve her children regularly. They learnt to measure, calculate, prep ingredients and built confidence with every triumphant and successful bake.

With her interest in baking and cooking, she regularly attended many baking and cooking courses.

These courses augmented her knowledge and experience and strengthened her network of local and overseas baking experts. In her year-long business incubation period, she put her commissions into a separate account intended for her business venture, secured agreements with a global network of baking instructors, explored locations for her baking studio, built a curriculum of popular recipes, planned exciting mother-child holiday programs, and secured sponsorships and endorsements.

When she launched her business, she also collaborated with digital marketing experts to manage her business presence online to generate awareness. Her business flourished.

What are your values?

Your values are your personal beliefs that are important to you and determine the way you live and work. When your life's activities are aligned with your values, you will feel content. This holds true for your work as well. This is too important to ignore as it could be a major source of internal dissonance.

For example, one of our clients identified fairness and teamwork as really important values at work. She expected to be fairly rewarded for her efforts and would also consistently give due credit to her colleagues. The company she worked for, however, had aggressive growth targets, and she noticed that the employees were being lauded and rewarded for aggressive sales tactics, questionable promises to clients, and even heavy-handed tactics to close deals. The last straw was when her client was hijacked by a co-worker from a different product group who offered a similar solution but with better terms. When she escalated this to her management, they responded by saying that it was her own fault for being outsmarted. She was extremely upset that the organization prized success over teamwork and fair play. She did not stay with that company for long.

It is important to articulate your value system clearly instead of leaving it as a poorly defined list of 'maybes'. What do you stand for? What do you stand against? What goes against the grain of your beliefs?

Here are some questions that you need to ask yourself.

Is the industry aligned to your values?

One of the key questions you need to answer is whether the industry you are in or are about to join has values that match yours. There are individuals who simply refuse to work in casinos, tobacco, chemicals, or even fast-food industries on principle as these industries go against their personal values.

One client rejected the opportunity to interview with a large soft drink company. For health reasons, she generally does not consume sugar-laden sodas and does not even allow sugary drinks at home. Despite the promise of an exciting role, she felt that it would be wrong to be employed by any soda manufacturer and decided to decline the opportunity.

What is your work-life equilibrium?

In today's pandemic-driven work-from-home (WFH) environment, work-life balance has become a major issue, evolving from merely 'balancing' work and personal life, to 'integrating' work *into* personal life. Many have not been able to draw boundaries, resulting in fatigue, exhaustion, and even burnout.

Do think about what your personal needs are and figure out your work boundaries.

Perhaps you are planning to have children in the near future, and if your work requires you to travel out of town frequently, you would have to be prepared to spend time away from them. Or perhaps your children are older and more independent, and you feel you can now focus on accelerating your career and take on more responsibilities. Some of our clients have put their careers on hold to look after an aging parent or to pursue further studies.

There are different formats of work today, from flexi-time to full-time work-from-home arrangements. Think about what is important to you, and then figure out how to fit in your work schedule and employment format.

How important is team dynamics?

Your values may be deeply personal but, sometimes, could extend to the people with whom you work. Does the boss or the team you work with share your values? Do they respect each other in an encouraging manner like you do?

A client once joined an extremely sales-driven organization where the business owner goaded his staff into spending commission cheques on luxury watches and even fancy cars, citing that it was their culture to show that they are successful. Our client realized that it wasn't just to flaunt their successes, but to insidiously force them to take on unnecessary debt so that they would have to work harder to pay off their credit card bills. He quit after 6 months citing 'toxic work culture' as his reason for leaving.

We also had a client whose boss insisted he escort his customers to questionable entertainment establishments, to ensure that he 'kept the customer happy'. This made him very uncomfortable and he decided to resign.

If your leader or team environment insists on behaviours that are opposed to your values, it usually results in discomfort and stress, which if prolonged, can result in mental distress.

Are corporate values important to you?

A company's values and its resulting actions can also impact your job satisfaction. Does the organization reflect the values you subscribe to? Is your company active in supporting the environment? Does it advocate respect for all?

A finance director refused to work for another family-run billion-dollar regional conglomerate ever again because they allegedly had three sets of accounts and made him sign-off on dubious statements and reports. He said, 'I wanted to be able to sleep at night. What they wanted me to do was against my principles'.

Real Career Stories: Yvonne, 33, Multi-level Sales Executive

Yvonne had a string of unfortunate work experiences. She hopped from one job to another without much success and was getting very frustrated until a close friend of hers recommended that she joined her 'multi-level marketing' organization as a 'member'. All she had to do was to sell 'healthy vitamin drinks' to her friends and make a hefty commission out of it.

It sounded interesting and she started with them, hitting her targets in the first 3 months.

However, her sales targets increased and the only way she could reach them was to sell 'memberships' to her friends to get them onboard to sell these products as her 'downstream'.

She then started to aggressively pitch to her friends, even those who couldn't afford the $5,000 'start-up fee', encouraging them to use their credit cards to make that payment. She was actually quite persuasive and managed to close her sales above her targets.

After a while, Yvonne realized that such behaviour was not congruent with her values and she was also feeling very exhausted. She realized that it was because pushing 'bad products and services' was not something she wanted for herself in the long run and resigned.

'Although I made a lot of money and felt I was "outwardly" successful, I did not feel enriched by the work that I did and I decided that it was not my true personality to be deceitful to others.'

Limitations and Gaps

Having identified all the elements that you want, you also have to consider if there are any constraints preventing you from achieving your dream career.

- In your new chosen career path, is further education, training, or certification required?
- What is the financial outlay of your decision to start a business?
- Is there a gap in your experience or skill sets that would prevent you from achieving your desired role?
- Does your new career choice pay enough for your chosen lifestyle?

Many senior executives have contemplated a pivot into academia, thinking, 'Now that I'm nearing retirement, I think I will go and teach.' Unfortunately, this move is not as straightforward as many think it is. Academic institutions have high entry requirements, like a master's degree or higher, pedagogy knowledge, actual teaching experience, and more. The pivot into academia may require more time than initially thought and would require a lot of advance preparation and planning.

Your personal self-assessment is useful, but you have to also research the marketplace in order to find out what the market needs. Having identified the gaps, the next steps involve making tangible plans towards achieving the necessary experiences or certifications to make a successful pivot.

Here is a simple template you can use to analyze your gaps and to plan your future actions:

Gaps	Why	Action Steps	Resources	Deadline
Insufficient formal training certification	as proof to the academic institution and builds credibility because they don't know my capabilities	Explore several training institutions. Get pricing. Attend information sessions. Ask for subsidies.	Speak to Mr A, Ms B, and Mr C for more information and advice.	Secure certification by Q4 this year.

You may also wish to work with a mentor or a coach who would hold you accountable and ensure that you take the necessary steps to attain your goal.

Personality

We have been asked by many clients whether personality plays a part in a career choice. There is some truth that people gravitate to roles and professions that fit their personalities but we know that there are many other factors that impact successful career choices. Certain professions require particular traits. For instance, nursing requires a caring, patient personality whereas accounting would require a meticulous nature with fine attention to detail. If you choose to enter or remain in a role or industry that does not fit your personality well, it could result in stress. For example, an introvert might find a cold-calling sales role exhausting as it requires a lot of interaction with strangers, whereas an extrovert might find a desk-bound auditing job intolerable in the long run. Even as you are conducting research about your dream job, we recommend that you find out whether there are any personality traits that would give you an innate advantage or disadvantage in that role.

Conclusion

In order to have a sustainable career that you can enjoy, a lot of research has to be conducted to find out what your ideal job looks like. Besides uncovering what you want more of and what you don't, it is important to know whether the personality requirements of the new role or values of the company are aligned to yours. Speak to individuals who are already in such roles and ask them if they think you would fit in. Only when you are armed with all this information will the risks involved in making a move be greatly reduced.

10

Career Crossroad Strategies

Many executives encounter one or more career crossroads during their working life. From our experience, we see that even successful business leaders with sterling careers experience this.

In this chapter, we will discuss the signs and the symptoms of a career crossroad. We will also explore the reasons why this happens, and most importantly, do a deep dive into some of the actions that you can take to make the crossroad experience less bumpy and achieve a positive outcome.

What is a career crossroad?

A career crossroad is a point when one faces multiple career options and needs clarity to make the right decisions. It could be an accountant wondering whether to pivot to a non-finance role or a director considering a competitor's offer to join them. We even had a client, who was a computer programmer, deciding whether to continue his passion as a coder or to move into a management function. From our experience, career crossroads can take many forms and often occur between the ages of 35 and 48.

What are some of the signs and symptoms?

Individuals encounter one or more of the following symptoms when they are at their career crossroad:

- 'Monday Morning Blues', a feeling of dread going to work on Monday mornings, or when thinking about the week ahead on Sunday evenings
- Questions like 'Where is my career heading?', 'What's next for me?' and 'Is this really what I want to do for the rest of my life?'
- Self-doubt and negative thoughts like 'I'm not sure if this role is right for me anymore'
- Looking through online Job Ads 'just to see what's out there'
- Thinking of quitting and starting your own business
- Losing sleep thinking about work

Very often, these career concerns are already lurking in the background, buried in the subconscious of busy executives, but because they are deluged with tight deadlines and demanding targets, they are too distracted to notice them, until a trigger event happens and, suddenly, all these concerns come to the forefront. These triggers could be an organization restructuring, a new boss, a health scare, or even a life-changing event.

A CEO of a multimillion-dollar online payment solutions company was perfectly happy with his successful corporate life until he was holidaying in Phuket in 2003 when the tsunami struck. Fortunately, he was on a boat when the waves came in and was largely unaffected, but he saw the utter devastation and loss of life that followed. He returned to Singapore, quit his job, and took a year-long sabbatical to reflect on his purpose in life. He created a technology start-up that was also a social enterprise and never looked back.

So, triggers can come in many forms, but when it strikes, it often affects the unprepared individual and causes them to make emotional responses. One such example was a disgruntled engineer we knew, who left his company with no job in hand and regretted it because it took him a very long time to find another similar role.

Why is it even more pressing now?

In today's disruptive economy, many of these triggers can happen anytime. External factors like the pandemic and fickle consumer demands can alter the market dynamics anytime, resulting in changes that happen so quickly and unexpectedly that there is no time to react. One wrong move could lead to repercussions that might take years to correct. That is why a working Career Strategy is needed for those who are at their career crossroad in order to respond to these changes effectively.

What to do when facing a career crossroad?

The worst thing to do at a career crossroad is to get emotional and make hasty decisions you might regret later. Pause, take a deep breath, and exhale. After you have calmed down, gather all the information regarding your Career Strategy from Chapters 5 and 6 to determine your next moves.

What's your career velocity? Do you want to accelerate, hover, or downshift? What's your career direction? Do you want to stay in your current role and industry or do you want to shift into another career quadrant? What's your career intent? Do you want to specialize, generalize, or create a new role for yourself? With this set of career strategies, you will have a better framework with which to evaluate your options.

Real Life Career Story: Joan, 41, Private Banker

Joan was a frustrated private banker. She had been servicing her ultra-rich clients for the past 11 years and she felt exhausted having to pander to them.

'I'm tired of working this job. The clients are too demanding, the colleagues are difficult to manage, the hours are long, and the boss is unreasonable. At least the pay is good.'

In exasperation, she quit her job in a haste and invested in a 'hipster café' along the East Coast. It cost her a lot of money to set it up and she was really happy running it for the first 6 months.

A year later, she shut the café down. When asked why, she candidly replied, 'I'm tired of running the business. The clients are too demanding, the staff are difficult to manage, the hours are exceedingly long, and the landlord is unreasonable . . . and the pay is really bad'.

Joan allowed her frustration to overtake her logic and made a hasty and emotional move which led to financial losses. 'Be careful of the shiny new ideas,' she cautioned. 'These may seem attractive to you, but in reality, are mere distractions from the right path to take.'

Defining Your Dream Job

Many executives come to us, desiring to land their 'dream job', but when pressed to define what their 'dream job' is, are unable to articulate it. 'A better paying job', 'a nicer boss', 'meaningful work', and 'better work-life balance' are some of the vague responses we get. The truth is, many are unable to verbalize their ideal vocation because they have not given it sufficient thought.

And if you are unable to clearly specify what you want, how would you know what to pursue? Or will you be leaving it to chance in a 'let's see what turns up' or a 'spray and pray' strategy that could result in less-than-ideal outcomes? This is where you will need to use the information from the previous chapter regarding your values. Knowing what you want more or less of and your skills and competencies can help determine what your dream job should look like. Putting it together, you will have greater clarity and be able to answer the question with a more specific response such as: 'My dream job would be a marketing role with a fast-growing high-tech company, managing a small team focused on developing digital assets in the region.'

Having such clarity will enable you to narrow the field of options and target the right opportunities.

Other Considerations at Your Career Crossroad

The decisions you make at your career crossroad will depend on many factors. Apart from your Career Strategy, here are some other things you will also need to consider.

What format of work to choose?

In today's world of work, the traditional 9 to 5 work arrangements seem to be a thing of the past. With technology aiding (or handicapping) the office worker, allowing them access to emails, messages, and videoconferencing even after office hours, does the concept of 'standard working hours' even apply anymore?

Similarly, the outlook on career advancement has also been redefined. What used to be seen as 'stepping down' is now seen as 'recalibration'.

For instance, it used to be taboo for high flying executives to decline promotions, but today, we see successful leaders being very selective of their upward mobility options, turning down bigger opportunities in favour of less stressful roles.

Likewise, the concept of 'contract work' used to be equated with 'temporary workers' doing transient work with no permanent attachment to the organization. Contractors were seen as 'outsiders' rather than employees. However, we argue that the only difference between contract work lasting for, say, 12 months compared to full-time employment is largely imaginary. Because organizations restructure all the time, there is no permanence to the employment contract, hence there is little difference from a fixed-term contract.

So, you may wish to consider short-term assignments as viable options as they could lead to greater exposure and possibly a conversion to something more permanent.

How about portfolio careers?

Another phenomenon we noticed that is gaining traction is the practice of having a portfolio career. In the traditional model of employment, workers used to hold on to one job with one company drawing one salary. Anything outside of that was considered moonlighting and was deeply frowned upon.

In the portfolio career model that many had chosen to undertake in the 'gig economy', individuals take on different jobs with different companies, drawing multiple income streams. In other words, they are holding on to a portfolio of jobs. This could be consulting projects for smaller companies, paid coaching sessions, lecturing at a local university, and/or being a board advisor for a start-up. These 'gigs' could take place at the same time or in succession—the choice depends on the client's timing or the individual's availability.

A client took our advice to embark on a portfolio career and ended up with a wonderfully aligned set of projects which resulted in a lucrative selection of roles that kept her busy and engaged. She enjoyed the flexibility of choosing projects which she loved and declining work from clients she felt might be unreasonable.

One key benefit of this model is the flexibility and control that allows you to focus on your priorities at that moment.

Real Life Career Story: Eunice, 39, Flexi Mom

Eunice was retrenched from her start-up company last December. The founders ran out of funding and had to let everyone go. Eunice was a skilled UI (user interface) Designer and built wonderful websites and applications for her company.

She had 2 young children, 4 and 8 years old and did not have any childcare support. She was contemplating 'retiring' to become a full-time mom and let her husband be the sole breadwinner.

Into the third month of her unemployment, her former boss, who had moved back to Germany, asked her if she could work remotely for him, but only for 3 days a week as they didn't need a full-time designer yet. She agreed as it gave her time to look after the family. The following month, a former colleague asked her to be their social media manager for a 6-month project. This project needed only 2 hours of work a day. As she had spare capacity on her hands, she agreed to accept it.

After that, she continued to take on ad hoc projects as long as she had the time to do it. This worked out well for her because she was now in full control of her working hours, was able to pick and choose the types of projects she loved, and also had time for her family.

'I feel I'm finally in control of my time and my career. Having a portfolio of jobs gives me the flexibility to be an effective professional and an effective mom.'

Which career quadrant to pivot to?

One of the most integral parts of your decision at your career crossroad would be which career quadrant you want to pursue. This will guide your decision as to which industries and roles you want to specifically target.

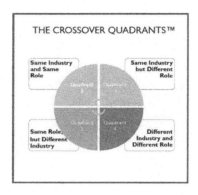

Without a map of where you want to focus your job search strategy on, your efforts would be diffused and the results unsatisfactory.

For instance, if you are a pediatric nursing manager in healthcare but wish to pivot into Quadrant 3 which is to remain in the medical industry but in a different role, then you could move into training and teach younger nurses how to handle babies. You will therefore need to target training or university hospitals to see if such programmes are being organized on a full-time basis. You might also need to get a trainer's certificate that will enable you to be recognized as a qualified instructor. You may also need to augment your technical knowledge with a course in instructional design so that you can create new curriculum to add more value to the new company.

Once you have decided which CAREER QUADRANT to pivot into, make plans to network and find out more about those roles, and start to take action!

'But I really don't know where to begin.'

We hear many executives who are at their career crossroads use this to explain their paralysis. They simply have no idea what the next steps are, let along decide on which pathway to choose.

Firstly, our advice is to understand and map out your Career Strategy. This should give you some basic clarity as to where you want to head.

Secondly and most importantly, you need to gather data. At the moment, you are stuck because you do not have much information about the industry or the role you have targeted, or are yet to target. There is plenty that you don't know, and even more that you *don't even know* that you don't know.

In order to make better decisions, you will have to gather data and form your own picture with it.

Reach out to people already in the industry and begin by asking them the following questions:

- What do you do?
- Who are the major players in your industry?
- Where is the growth in your industry coming from?
- What are the obstacles or disruptions ahead?
- What skills or roles are in short supply in your sector?
- What advice can you give me if I were to join your industry?
- Is there someone I could speak with to learn more?

This process takes time, so do not expect immediate results. Each person you meet amplifies your understanding of the role and industry, so try to meet and speak with as many as possible.

Making the Mid-career Switch

If you are considering a Quadrant 4 move (to a different industry and in a different role), you are intending to make a complete 'mid-career switch'.

For example, a banker who resigns to start a sports training business for children, or a HR Manager who quits to join a bicycle components company as their general manager.

Quadrant 4 moves are inherently risky and that is why we advise a deep and hard look before making the leap. You will need to ask yourself these 5 questions.

Why?

One of the simplest questions to ask yourself is whether this is an emotional or rational decision. Is it borne out of haste or have you been thinking about this for a long time? What is your biggest career problem? Can you articulate it? How real is it? Will resigning from your job and switching into a totally different role and industry solve it? Sometimes, your problem could be a temporary one, like 'I have a new boss who hates me,' which could be resolved as the working relationship improves over time.

Am I ready?

If you have decided to make a mid-career switch, another tough question to ask is whether you are emotionally and financially prepared for the journey ahead. A switch like this is never easy. It takes time and you might even face a reduction in or absence of a salary. Do you have enough money to ride through the transitional phase? It might take as long as 18 months for things to stabilize—do you have the resources to weather this challenging period?

The hours involved in a mid-career switch could also be very long, given the steep learning curve and new skills to master. It will be emotionally draining, sometimes even more so than your previous role. Are you equipped with the emotional resilience needed? How about your spouse or partner? We have seen many plans fall apart due to lack of spousal or partner support. Do not be part of that statistic. Have an open and mature conversation and plan the future together.

How do I get there?

Once you have decided which industry/role to target, the next question is 'How do I get there?'

Having a general idea is a good start to your mid-career switching journey, but it is only the beginning. You will need to take action to get to your destination. Begin by asking yourself the following questions:

- Am I qualified? If not, how do I get the qualifications I need?
- Am I sufficiently skilled to make an impact, or am I merely 'good enough'? What will it take for me to master these skills?
- Do I have enough information about the role or the industry? Are these fact-based or assumptions that I am making? Is my data accurate and up to date? Are my sources reliable? You do not want to premise your critical career decisions on hearsay.
- Do these hiring managers even know me? How do I get myself noticed? What are the transferable skills I've mastered over the years that can help them solve their current business challenges?

Are you still relevant to the market?

For some individuals who have not been upgrading their skills and knowledge for the longest time, they might find their skillsets becoming irrelevant. This does not apply only to the senior or older employees, we have also seen 30-somethings with skillsets that are no longer relevant to the market.

If you think that your skills have become obsolete, you might have to either reskill or start right back at the bottom with a total career reboot.

Our client who was a 38-year-old bookkeeper realized that balancing ledgers is all automated now and she took the painful step of retraining as a data analyst instead. It was really challenging but she eventually secured a junior analyst role and is now on her way to getting promoted at her new company.

Conclusion

Managing your career crossroads can seem very daunting and scary, with so many things that could go wrong. This fear could freeze us into inaction, making us kick the can down the road to face it again at some future date. When you encounter a career crossroad, pause, formulate a plan and then take action. Some challenges are better resolved today. Instead of quitting your job in a rage and desperately hunting for a role the day after, give yourself a time-frame—say, 6 months—to put together a Career Strategy. This will give you more time and information regarding your options and you can make your own moves towards these opportunities. Take baby-steps and try not to bite off more than you can chew. Whatever you do, never rush headlong into this.

Of course, engaging an experienced career strategist to help with your career crossroad challenges is always a great idea as it will reduce the risks and speed up your learning curve.

11

Accelerating Your Career

If you have determined your Career Strategy, you might now be thinking about how to fast-track your career or boost your career trajectory. If you're wondering how to get that promotion or if you want to take on more responsibilities, then this chapter was written especially for you.

Career Acceleration

Career acceleration refers to the act of shifting your focus to progress your career—to gain greater responsibility, earn a higher income, and attain more authority and influence. Professionally, that also means enhancing and elevating your skills and expertise and take on greater responsibilities.

Those who are looking at accelerating their careers need to be aware that things don't always 'just happen'. Sometimes we hear people say things like this: 'John was promoted last week. He is always so lucky to be at the right place at the right time!'

There is a flawed belief that these people are merely born lucky, as though things happen fortuitously without any human intervention. In reality, career acceleration requires a significant amount of awareness, emotional quotient, planning, and innate curiosity and interest about the work, the market, and the people in the business. Some individuals are natural at this but for most of us, some effort is required. Career acceleration requires time, strategy, and patience.

In this chapter, we will focus on career acceleration *within one's own organization*, i.e., getting promoted internally as this requires more planning and thought than simply applying for a larger role with another company.

Why do you want to accelerate?

Before you consider accelerating your career, you should think about your 'why?'. Is it for personal development? If so, which areas and why?

Our client, a Sales Manager, as part of his acceleration strategy, expanded his job scope to include some marketing functions so that he could learn even more about the business.

Or are you planning to accelerate your career for more money or status? A promotion usually brings with it an increase in salary and a more prestigious title.

Having determined your reasons, you have to now figure out if your acceleration strategy fits with your Career Strategy and your life strategy.

What is acceleration?

There is a common misconception that career acceleration *only* involves a promotion—an elevation in job title and salary. It is often seen as taking over your boss' job. But in today's flat organizations, you might have to wait a very long time for your direct boss to retire or leave before you can take over, and by that time, that position may not even exist.

Our advice is not to be short-sighted and getting distracted by the shiny little things. The focus of career acceleration is not just title or money, but career progression in terms of growth of your professional skills, expertise, and knowledge. It could also encompass an increase in influence, respect, and authority you have within your organization.

As such, taking on a larger role that gives you more exposure to the company's operations and increases your exposure to senior management still counts as career progression.

You might be given new responsibilities or a larger scope without a bigger job title, but it is still beneficial as you add new experiences and achievements to your career story. Making lateral moves can even help your career in a complex environment. Sometimes, you might need to take a step back or a lateral shift in order to move forward. This is necessary when you lack the required experience and undertaking a smaller role for a period of time could help you gain the network, skills, and experience to propel yourself forward.

If the opportunity arises, you might want to take on a smaller scope with a fast-growing team or with an up-and-coming leader. Whilst this may seem like taking one step backwards, in reality, it's a springboard for you to pivot your career into an adjacent space and, from there, you could hop three steps forward.

Real Life Career Story: Charles, 35, The Career Accelerator
Charles was a Sales Manager with a mid-sized pharmaceutical company and he was looking to accelerate his career. He actively applied for sales director positions, but the roles that were advertised were with smaller organizations, or with products companies that were not aligned to his career interests. The organizations that he was interested in, however, were not hiring.

Feeling increasingly frustrated, he spoke with us and shared his desire for better career prospects.

As his company was actually in aggressive growth mode, we told him to consider bigger roles within his organization that would be interesting for him and also in line with his current skillsets as a sales manager.

He had a conversation with his bosses and HR and together, they identified a sales planning and operations manager role that had just opened up. Even though it was at the same job grade and was regarded as a lateral move, he successfully interviewed for it.

In that role, he learnt new skills and widened his experience. He even initiated several new programs that led to increased efficiencies. Because of his strong performance in this role, he was promoted a year later to head the regional sales operations function.

'I learnt that sometimes, you don't shoot for a bigger title or paygrade. Sometimes, you move into a role first, prove yourself, then get promoted.'

Are you ready to accelerate?

Are you mentally, emotionally, and physically ready for the increase in responsibilities? Do you have the requisite skills? What is your current life-stage and do you have the ability to handle the extra work?

Before deciding to accelerate, you will need to ensure that you are prepared for the long slog ahead. We have seen executives who felt they were ready but their home situations were not ideal for a larger role taking up more of their time at that moment, as illustrated in the following case study.

Real Life Career Story: Dr Eric Smith, 36, The Eye Surgeon
Dr Smith was an eye surgeon who was approached for a corporate role with a healthcare company. The opportunity was an exciting one involving travel that took up almost 70% of his time, covering markets all over Asia.

The compensation was also attractive as there were generous benefits, share options, and performance bonuses. He was very keen to take on the role as he had grown tired of his work at the clinic and had lost his passion for medical practice. At first glance, this career acceleration opportunity looked like it was a straightforward one.

But the story gets complicated. Eric was married with 3 young children. Moreover, his wife was an emergency room surgeon whose hours were unpredictable and was regularly called to emergencies at any time of the day or night. They had not had much luck with childcare support and had changed nannies 3 times in 2 years.

After much soul searching, he realized taking on a new job with additional stress and extensive travel may just be too much for his family and he decided to decline the offer.

'I felt I was not ready for a bigger role and I chose to put my family first instead of my career.'

Today, Dr Smith is still running his thriving medical practice and has a very happy family.

Ten Strategies to Accelerate Your Career

If you are considering accelerating your career, here are some considerations.

#1	• See the big picture
#2	• Watch for trends
#3	• Scan for internal opportunities
#4	• Manage your stakeholders
#5	• Curate your brand and reputation
#6	• Build your strategic network
#7	• Build trust
#8	• Stay visible and connected
#9	• Get mentors and sponsors
#10	• Develop executive presence

Strategy #1: See the Big Picture

What makes your CEO and senior leaders stand out from the rest of the employees and just how did they get there in the first place?

It is because they are able to take a step back and see the big picture.

Often, we are so busy watching our little patch of business that we overlook the bigger picture. Do you know what is happening in the other divisions within your organization? What are the current issues being faced by the other business units? What are your competitors doing?

To accelerate your career, you should consider your leader's point of view and align yours to it. How can you create more value for the shareholders? What can be done to create sustainable value for the company? Centre your ideas around these themes and drive the business towards these goals rather than just on your immediate KPIs.

Your activities and achievements will be noticed by the leadership team and you will be on their radar for future senior roles.

Strategy #2: Watch for Trends

You need to develop awareness of the marketplace as it is critical in figuring out how your industry is doing. Are there emerging technologies that may change the way work is done? Are there disruptions on the horizon? What about new opportunities you or your organization should leverage? Perhaps you have noticed an interesting trend and may want to nudge your organization in that direction.

For instance, if you are in IT, is there a cheaper and more effective cloud or automation solution that could save your company millions of dollars? If so, get more research done and champion this blockbuster initiative.

Sometimes, companies also work on special projects for new products or markets. Find out how you can get on these high-profile projects to learn more about these new technologies and models. There is a lot of career progression potential there.

Strategy #3: Scan For Internal Opportunities

Sometimes, we overlook the obvious opportunities to progress internally. Look inside your organization and analyze the talent situation. Are there skill gaps in other divisions that you can fill? Is it possible for you to help another high-profile team in some way? How can you get on their radar so that they would appreciate your inputs and insights?

Another area to keep an eye on is planned staff movements in the next 6 to 12 months.

Was there someone who has recently retired, resigned, or was promoted? Is there now a gap that you can possibly fill? What exactly are they looking for in a replacement and how do you get on the radar of the hiring manager? If your organization practices succession planning, are you in any of these talent pipelines? You have to figure out whom to speak with to indicate your interest.

Strategy #4: Manage Your Stakeholders

Many careers have been derailed due to poor stakeholder management. Managing upwards is a skill that needs to be learned and honed. In a complex organizational structure, multiple stakeholders need to be engaged and sometimes, placated at the same time. Although there is a ton of advice and books regarding the strategies to manage upwards, we want to share a few practical tips that you can immediately put to practice.

See the boss' perspective.

To manage up more effectively, you must understand your boss' agendas, goals, personality, and needs. Try to view the business through your boss' filter. As you imagine yourself in their place, think about what problems and challenges are foremost on their minds. Then, think about how you can help solve them.

Sometimes, your own agenda may not align with theirs. For instance, a sales executive's primary KPI is to drive top-line revenues, so he lowers his prices and gives 90-day credit terms to get maximum sales. However, his boss' KPI might actually be margin-driven and prompt collection of receivables, so the more the executive sells, the more difficult the boss' job becomes.

Think like your boss and help him achieve what he needs. Try to take on additional tasks or responsibilities that would ease his burden or make him look good to his stakeholders.

Raise your 'business value'.

To get promoted, you need to create a lot more value than what you are tasked to do. For instance, as a finance manager, you may be assessed on how accurate and timely your reporting is, but those factors are exactly what you are paid to do. Instead, focus on larger strategic issues like 'How do I increase the cashflow of the company?' or 'Is there a cheaper source of funds we can access to save money?'. By operating one level above what you are paid to do, you are demonstrating to senior management that you can be trusted with bigger responsibilities when the opportunity arises.

Communicate regularly.

Keep your bosses and key stakeholders updated on your key activities and achievements regularly. Stay in the forefront of their sphere of attention so that you are always on their radar. Communicate your goals and actions clearly and regularly, and should any mistakes happen, inform them before they hear about it from someone else.

Generally, it's important to keep your bosses updated on your activities and to ensure that they know all the important news—both good and bad. This helps them manage the other stakeholders in the business as well.

Stakeholder Management Quadrant for Effective Communication

In any large, complex bureaucracy, there are multiple stakeholders to manage. It's not just about your direct supervisor. You have to also consider the personalities and agendas of the senior business leaders and the heads of other business functions as well.

Here is a basic Stakeholder Management Matrix.

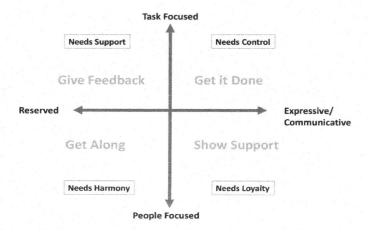

On the vertical axis, we identified the leader as being 'task-focused' on one end and 'people-focused' on the other. The task-focused leader is unlikely to need small talk and would probably prefer that you get to the point. The people-centric leader would most likely have a keen interest in how you are doing and would probably appreciate it if you showed some interest in his/her well-being, too.

The horizontal spectrum ranges from 'reserved' to 'expressive'. Some individuals express their every thought, while others prefer not to talk too much. The reserved leader is less likely to be communicative, so you might have to find a good time to speak about important matters.

At the top right quadrant, the task-focused and expressive leaders need you to get your job done and is likely to make it very clear to the team what and how the work needs to be done. They would welcome questions and clarifications, and you will generally always know where you stand and what their expectations are.

Task-focused but reserved leaders (top left quadrant) may not be entirely clear on their expectations, so you may have to find alternative ways to clarify things. Emails or 1-to-1 catch-ups are highly recommended.

People-focused leaders who are expressive (bottom right quadrant) will probably be easy to get along with. Do demonstrate your support and loyalty explicitly and get your job done.

People-focused leaders who are reserved (bottom left quadrant) may not express their expectations clearly and are most likely not delegating as much as they should. They value harmony and prefer that the team gets along and resolve their own problems. Do initiate regular catch-ups to keep them updated.

Having described all the quadrants, your task now is to map your own stakeholders to this model—where would your boss fit? What about the other business heads you frequently work with? Map them all and think about their communication preferences and management styles. Doing this would help you prepare for future conversations better.

Strategy #5: Curate Your Brand and Reputation

Real Life Career Story: Jolene, 38, The Digital Guru
Whenever there was a problem with anything that had to do with online sales, search engine optimization, or digital marketing, everyone in the organization knew who to call: Jolene, the Digital Guru.

And why not? After all, she had successfully launched the e-commerce platform for the company that led to 9x sales growth, and everyone remembers how she implemented the customer self-service kiosks that increased client satisfaction by 300%!

It didn't matter that Jolene had a basic degree in Geology, or that she had started her career in the warehouse. Today, she is known for the string of technology projects she designed and implemented which improved the business significantly.

She is constantly in demand for all major projects.

It has been said that it is not about who you know, but about who knows you and what you're known for. Hence, building your reputation in your company is critical in helping you with your career acceleration. Whether people seek your expertise when they need a particular skill for the next big project or if they avoid working with you because you're known to be inflexible, your reputation decides whether you get ahead in the organization or not. If you are consistently late for work or meetings, you will end up building a reputation for being poor at time management or perceived as unable to keep up with the workload. As a result, no one would choose to work with you. However, if you're already doing great work and delivering on your tasks and contributing actively to corporate success, then you're building the necessary reputation that will get you noticed for future promotions.

Focus on what you want to be known for and ensure your work behaviours and results reinforce those qualities. Display visible values, enthusiasm, and engagement consistently.

Strategy #6: Build Your Strategic Network

We all know the benefits of networking, but how many of us enjoy doing it, or even understand how to do it correctly? Having a wide network helps you remain up to date with what is happening in the market, allowing you to predict future trends or threats to your industry so that you can be better prepared.

Effective networking is a mindset of 'giving' rather than 'taking'. Express genuine curiosity about your network's business, industry, and personal and professional challenges. You may be surprised by what you learn. Go out to meet people without the expectations of getting something from them in return. True networking is a two-way street. As you help others, others will return you the favour and you can ask them for advice in return, or even for a favour in the future.

Real Life Career Story: Melvin, 44, Operations Director
Melvin had over 20 years of experience in product manufacturing when he reached his career crossroads. His new boss was difficult and exacting and he started to dread going to work, wondering if he should make a career pivot into something else that was more exciting. As head of operations, he conducted many trainings on protocols, quality, compliance, and operations processes and was curious whether he could translate that into a career in teaching.

He reached out to his network of academic contacts and had several conversations. Fortuitously, one lead surfaced for a role as an adjunct lecturer in a technical field and because he was referred by a contact who was quite senior in the institution, the HR leaders arranged for an interview.

During the interview, it became clear that he had significant gaps in his background. He felt that he could have done the job if given the opportunity, but the hiring leaders needed to find an individual with credibility that would immediately command the respect of their students. They were looking for relevant past experience not just in conducting academic classes, but in setting assignments, establishing grading rubrics, setting exam questions, and more.

However, because the business leader who recommended Melvin knew him personally and was able to vouch for his effectiveness in training, the organization was willing to give him a chance and made him an offer. Today, he is doing extremely well in that role and has been promoted twice. 'Sometimes, progressing in your career isn't about who you know, but rather, who knows you.'

When we develop our networking strategy, we must consider two components:

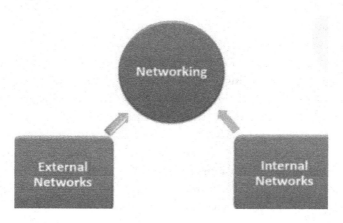

External networks

Regardless of your career direction, whether you're accelerating, downshifting, or hovering, it is important to maintain a strong external network so that you know what's going on with the extended business world. You will reinforce your position as a valuable member of your current organization if you know what is happening in the industry and can advise your organization and senior leaders accordingly.

As a downshifter, your extended network would be helpful for your business assignments or projects.

Even if things are status quo in your career, your extended network could provide you with information to help you be more effective in your work and to pre-empt any impending industry disruptions.

Examples of external networks could include your business partners, suppliers, vendors, consultants, or even your client's customers.

A simple habit you can adopt is to get out of the office once a week to catch up with an external contact. These should include people from outside your industry. Spread your net wide and make it a habit to reach out to new people to learn new things and build new relationships. Even though networking might be more difficult in a post-Covid world, Zoom networking is fast replacing the face-to-face meetings, so start to get comfortable with it. If an industry event is looming, actively reach out to your contacts so that you can meet up at the virtual event.

Internal networks

One area often neglected is networking within the organization. Some people think of this as office politics, but it's really about ensuring your visibility and reinforcing your reputation. Internal networking helps you learn about what the other divisions are doing, and in return, allows you to share more about your specific area of expertise to the other teams, helping them understand your business. This can smoothen the path for future collaborations. It helps build trust and earns you more credibility in the organization.

Your internal network includes the executives from other functions such as sales, marketing, operations, HR, finance, your counterparts in other countries, and senior management.

Internal networking is not as difficult as it seems and doesn't need to be forced. Most companies have corporate events such as conferences and social events like corporate social responsibility programs, team-bonding activities and informal get-togethers. Do make an effort to attend or even volunteer to organize such events. It would increase your visibility significantly as you now have access to colleagues and business leaders from other parts of the organization. Remember to reinforce your messaging, especially with key influencers. Let them know who you are, what you do, and your claim to fame (e.g. 'I was the one who closed the XYZ deal last month.') so they have anchors with which to remember you.

If you are actively networking, do attempt to keep a record or a tracking system of what was discussed in case you forget. With our busy lives, we will otherwise forget what was discussed.

Strategy #7: Build Trust

Nothing is more disappointing than not fulfilling a promise. When we make promises to our teammates and break them, we lose credibility and are seen to be unreliable. Done often enough, you will be branded as untrustworthy which is detrimental to your reputation within the organization. Start by keeping your smallest promises, like meeting agreed deadlines. Trust is the currency in any organization and the more trust you build and accumulate, the more influential you become.

Strategy #8: Stay Visible and Connected while Working from Home

Hybrid work environments are now more common than ever. In the era before Covid-19, you could arrange for lunch or step out for a quick coffee with your colleagues and engage them socially. Today, with work-from-home options being more readily accepted, networking effectively may be even harder than before.

We suggest that you build stronger bonds, actively seek out opportunities to connect with selected colleagues and bosses to get to know them better. These pockets of interactions generate goodwill, regardless of whether you are working virtually from home or physically at the office.

With reference to online meetings, one important thing to note is that your appearance matters as much as when meeting in person. While dressing casually is acceptable, appearing slovenly is not. It's akin to leaving your home to run errands in your underwear. You should make an effort to appear professional in all your online meetings.

It is also not professional to switch off your camera while in an online meeting. You may choose to mute yourself if you're not speaking but you should show yourself on camera. Look alert and participate actively in the conversation so that your stakeholders can observe your consistent enthusiasm and interest; in turn, they will respond better to you when you reach out to them to discuss business ideas or strategies in the future.

**Real Life Career Story: Crouching Tigers,
Hidden Dragons**

In an online leadership training we conducted last year during the pandemic, we did a presentation for a group of 28 mid to senior-level executives via Zoom. Surprisingly, more than half declined to turn their videos on and preferred to sit back and not interact at all, despite our requests to them to do so.

A highlight of the training was a guest appearance by one of their company's highest ranking VP who took time off her busy schedule halfway across the globe to give a short talk and answer questions.

Remarkably, the half that did not turn their videos on kept their videos off during this important segment! Besides being highly disrespectful to a senior leader, they lost an important opportunity to be seen and recognized by someone who could be instrumental in influencing their promotional prospects.

We also observed that she was paying particular attention to the participants who had their videos turned on and who were actively engaging her with good questions. We are most certain that they left a strong impression on the leader.

Zoom meetings are great opportunities to be seen, heard, and noticed by those who matter to your career prospects. Do not squander this golden opportunity.

Strategy #9: Get Mentors and Sponsors

As you grow in your career, take on fresh responsibilities and develop skills, having someone to guide you and 'show you the ropes' can be really helpful to shorten the learning curve. Seek out mentors with different competencies who can best advice you on a variety of issues. Business mentors can hail from any industry. As business leaders, they can advise you on business and professional matters. In your career, you might be offered interesting opportunities which can be complex, and having an objective voice might be helpful.

Real Life Career Story: Mike, 43, The Superstar

Mike feels he was born lucky. With an outgoing personality and likable demeanour, he was always seen as Mr Popular. So when he joined a big law firm, he was quickly taken under the wings of a partner who mentored him and took a personal interest in developing his career.

He likewise played the role of 'Protégé Extraordinaire' and went above and beyond what his role demanded in making sure his sponsor received all the support he needed.

The trust built up to a level where he always wanted Mike on all his high-profile cases.

Several years later, his sponsor was poached to join an even larger firm as a senior partner and he took Mike along with him, giving him a bigger title and salary. In that new firm, he was seen as a rising star and Mike's own star rose along with his.

Mike stayed under his umbrella for 18 years and even as he was fast approaching retirement age, he was still grooming Mike to take over his stable of top clients once he hung up his boots.

'I never knew I would stay with my mentor for so many years and I found that I learned a lot from him. My professional growth would not have been this accelerated had I tried to figure everything out on my own. I also learned that sponsorship is a two-way street and as his protégé, I had to bring all my skills, knowledge, and energy to make him an even better lawyer. So you can say that it was a symbiotic relationship we both benefited from.'

You can have mentors from all age groups and functions. There is no one person who would have all the answers to your career questions. Your mentor could even be a younger person who is more updated on the trends and can give you insights on the market. What is the difference between a mentor and a sponsor? A mentor has technical skills that you could learn and benefit from. They can help you with blind spots and guide you through difficult decisions, challenging tasks, and strategy design. A sponsor is someone highly placed in the organization who can expedite your career journey. They can help promote you to other leaders within the organization, raising your profile and reinforcing your reputation. Sometimes, these terms are used interchangeably, and mentors can become sponsors and vice versa.

What you should focus on is how to learn and get the best advice from the best people.

Strategy #10: Develop Executive Presence

Did you know that how you present yourself affects 70% of your promotion prospects? What your direct boss thinks of you and the impression your senior leaders have of you will directly affect whether you get that promotion. One of the key secrets to getting promoted is to inspire the confidence of your senior management. Things will be smoother for you when you engage them or even socialize with them. Your executive presence involves much more than how you are dressed. In this section, we will breakdown all the elements that to add to your executive presence.

Self-awareness and seeking feedback

Do you know your strengths and your blind spots? You have probably done several 360-degree feedback exercises in your career.

Has anyone given you accurate feedback on your brand and your weaknesses? Because you may not always get the full picture from formal feedback mechanisms, we recommend actively seeking feedback from your mentors and your colleagues. Ask for suggestions and advice, but do not focus on just the negatives. From there, build up your development plan and set targets.

Composure

The way you compose yourself can also send signals to those around you. Control your emotions and measure your responses. Be restrained, firm, and confident. Never lose control of your feelings in front of another person.

Many of us have experienced emotional bosses who yell at their staff when things go wrong, but this merely signals their lack of self-control. Outbursts like these never inspire confidence.

Watch your posture and your body language as well. Stand upright and move with intent. Former President Barrack Obama is the epitome of good executive presence. Make eye contact, pay attention, and actively listen when you are in a conversation. Listen carefully, wait a beat, and then respond. Do not react or take things personally and always pay attention to your tone.

Communication

Whether we like it or not, we are always being observed and judged by those around us, even those who are not physically in the office. They will make their own inferences based on the way you write emails or communicate on internal collaboration tools like Slack or Teams.

How you write reflects on you. Do not take shortcuts, use colloquialism or foul language in professional messages as you never know when your message might be forwarded to senior management. Be careful with sensitive topics like religion, politics, or even sports as you never know whom you might offend.

Confidence

To get promoted, you need to inspire confidence in those around you. Instill confidence in your leaders that you are a safe pair of hands to leave the business with. A confident demeanour assures your colleagues that you can support them as a reliable and steadfast team player and be the leader that your subordinates want to follow. So, we need to project confidence in the way we present ourselves.

When speaking with someone, be mindful not to use limiting words such as 'I think', 'Maybe', 'Perhaps', 'I could be wrong but . . .' as these phrases suggest self-doubt, the arch-enemy of self-confidence. Be resolute in your language and have faith in your decisions and others will return that level of faith.

Always be mindful of your speech and body language as it conveys the level of confidence you have.

Dress the part

One of the visual cues that determine a person's first impression of you is the way you are dressed. Dress appropriately for work. Be mindful of the professional image you need to project. Would you trust an eye surgeon who is scheduled to perform a LASIK surgery on your eyes if he walked into the clinic slovenly dressed with food-stains on his T-shirt?

Real Life Career Story: Alex, 40, The Misunderstood Clown

Alex was a strong performer in his team. He had been with the company, a strategy consultancy firm, for over 8 years and his performance could be described as above average. Jovial, loud, and recognizable by his signature hearty laughter, he had a quip for every situation and made everybody laugh. He was very popular with the team and the clients loved him. People often said, 'You can hear Alex before you see Alex. Yes, he is larger than life'.

He had been recommended for promotion three times in the past four years but never managed to land the coveted position.

He was confused as he had achieved all his targets and he felt the promotion was long overdue. One evening, he had a serious heart-to-heart with his manager about why he kept getting bypassed for leadership roles and the manager told him something that shocked him deeply.

'The senior leadership simply do not trust that you can be serious enough or have the gravitas to command the respect of the teams and clients. People love you, Alex, and view you as the "morale booster" of the group, but they see you more as a "buddy", not as the "boss". The leaders in HQ don't see the hard work and great results you bring in, but what they see during global meetings at HQ is a jester looking for attention, cracking jokes, and making people laugh. Until you can behave in a more serious fashion, people will continue to find it difficult to follow your lead.'

Conclusion

Career acceleration takes more than being at the right place at the right time. In this chapter, we have shared many practical strategies that, when implemented well, can boost your career trajectory.

Part F

Job Hunting Strategies

12

Landing Your Dream Job

Real Career Stories: Tricia, 39, Account Manager

Tricia was desperately in need of a new job. She had spent the last 9 years in a company where she was relatively happy until a new boss was parachuted in from the UK after a vicious political battle in her department, which resulted in her managers being fired. Even though she was not personally involved in the fracas, she was seen by the new boss as being part of the 'Old Guard' and he was making things difficult for her.

However, she couldn't quit without a job in hand as she needed the money to pay for her elderly parents' medical bills, so she endured the hostility.

She scoured various job boards and applied for close to 70 jobs and received only 4 calls from the advertisers. She could not understand why the response rate was so bad and figured that it must be her CV that was at fault. So, she paid a CV-writing service $500 for an updated version, but the response was equally dismal.

After 6 months of extensive applying and numerous disappointments, she started to think, 'If it's not the CV, then it must be me! I'm not marketable. There is something wrong with me'. These negative thoughts, together with her difficult work conditions, started her down a path of depression.

> She engaged us and after a thorough analysis of her situation, we found that it was not her profile that was wrong, but rather, her methodology. As she had not needed to look for a job for over a decade, she did not know how to job-hunt properly. She had been applying to jobs that were weeks old or were at the inappropriate levels for her. Some were even in industries she had no experience in. Her lack of job-search strategy was setting her up for failure.
>
> After learning how to be more precise in her focus and positioning from us, she landed a good job with a hefty salary increase. 'If only I knew all this from the very start!' she said.

As an integral part of career management, understanding the job search methodology is critical. This opportunity generating activity is key to progressing your career externally into new and exciting roles with other companies. Even if you are doing well in your current role, it is a good habit to keep an eye on the market for opportunities that align with your Career Strategy so that you can have the option of moving into more exciting roles.

We have dedicated this entire chapter on how you can land your dream job.

Why Traditional Methods of Job Search are Broken

For many years, the usual way of job hunting has been looking at job advertisements and sending your resume to the advertiser. This method is no longer effective. Today, with everyone being well connected, when there is a job vacancy, the first thing a hiring manager would do to find a suitable replacement is by word-of-mouth. He will certainly ask for referrals from among his team, friends, and professional network. This method is so effective that almost 80% of positions are filled this way.

As a result, there is little need to advertise for vacancies. Even for roles that are advertised, they may not be genuine opportunities. Many of the positions you might see online may have already been filled, meaning that the hiring manager has already decided who they want to offer the position to. Sometimes, the vacancy is posted online as an exercise to see if there are any better candidates in the market. The likelihood of the company hiring from the pool of external applicants would be extremely low as they probably do not have the bandwidth to filter through all the applications and are already progressing the preferred candidate through all the interviews.

So, even though you may fit the requirements of the role perfectly, no one is contacting you because of the sheer volume of applications. From our experience, every online advertisement generates an average of 300 applications per day and it is humanly impossible to review them all. Moreover, for each advertised job, you are competing against dozens of candidates vying for the role, many of whom are equally as qualified as you are. Hence, your chances of landing an interview decreases even more.

In our years of head-hunting, we have also encountered job advertisements for non-existent positions by unscrupulous recruiters who are out to collect profiles for their database. This leads to another dead end.

Our biggest argument against the traditional method of job hunting is that applying for jobs via online advertisements is far too passive.

There is a hidden job market, representing almost 80% of all job opportunities at any point in time which are not advertised. You need a well-planned job search strategy to yield good results from your efforts. Let's evaluate how we could do this better by discussing these following 7 strategies of job hunting.

#1	• Only target the right jobs
#2	• Be proactive, not reactive
#3	• Position yourself correctly
#4	• Interview strategically
#5	• Don't depend on recruiters
#6	• Leverage the power of LinkedIn
#7	• Take control of your campaign

Strategy #1: Only target the 'right' jobs.

If you don't know what you're aiming for, you're probably not going to hit it.

Are you just spraying and praying?

We encountered a frustrated executive who said, 'I sent out 200 resumes last month and got no response! The market is very bad!'

We replied, 'If you really sent out 200 resumes, you are not applying for jobs, you are *spamming*'.

Many times, job seekers visit a job portal, do a keyword search for the role they want, then hit the 'GO' button, and go crazy clicking on the 'Apply' button for every job opening they see, regardless of whether the role fits them or not.

Are you one of them?

We highly recommend curbing your enthusiasm and reserving your job applications for those you stand a good chance at landing.

Are you targeting the right roles?

One of our clients, a 42-year-old Sales Manager wanted to pivot into a CFO (Chief Finance Officer) role. He had an accounting degree but never practiced a day of finance management since he had graduated. He started applying for every CFO role he could find, despite not meeting the specified requirements. Even with a strong background in numbers and finance, he lacked the actual finance experience required for the role.

Needless to say, he never got any interviews.

A more reasonable approach for our client would be to target a lateral role, say in sales operations where he could gain more budgeting and planning experience first, then leverage that experience to move into finance. Relying on his industry expertise and knowledge, he can pivot into finance in a more structured way. Applying for a CFO role directly was unlikely to get him any response.

The right thing to do is to strategically target roles that fit your profile and which can give you the experience needed to fulfill your future ambitions.

Real Career Stories: John, 36, Chemical Engineer

John was trained as a chemical engineer and had spent 10 years with a top chemicals company. Even though he had strong technical skills, the last 4 years were spent as a change management specialist in the company, implementing new programs for different teams, in different business units across Asia.

His role was to understand what each business unit leader needed, translate the requirements into a document, then liaise with the external consultants to ensure the correct solution is designed. He then had to monitor the projects and was responsible for delivering them according to the deadlines set.

'I was playing the role of internal consultant and I loved it! I can see myself doing this with a top consultancy firm like McKinsey, Bain, or the Boston Consulting Group,' he said.

So, he started submitting unsolicited applications to these big firms, confident that they would hire him. However, he never received any responses. He then spoke to a friend who was in the consultancy industry and was told bluntly, 'Let's face it. You're a chemical engineer turned project manager, not the top-tier management consultant we would be looking for. Moreover, you don't even have an MBA. It's no wonder that nobody paid any attention to your CV. I'd suggest you fine-tune your expectations and aim for something more realistic'.

John shared, 'The feedback was painful, but true. I was applying for fantasy jobs rather than realistic ones. This helped me fine-tune my job search strategy greatly'.

Are you using the job sites correctly?

For those who use job sites exclusively for their searches, are you taking the necessary steps to improve your chances?

Check Recent Postings

A client once complained that he never received any responses for roles that he applied for, even though he felt he was the perfect fit for them. We asked him to show how he did it and we realized that he had been sorting his search results based on 'Relevance' rather than 'Recency' and was applying for roles that were over a month old.

As a rule of thumb, submit your application within 3 days of the advertised date as this window gives you the best advantage in terms of visibility. Better still, do it on the day the advertisement is posted. Never hold off until the closing date as your application would be right at the bottom of the pile. The recruiter who filters applications would probably not even look at your profile.

If you are actively job hunting, you should check the job portals regularly (and we mean daily) and have the appropriate version of your resume ready, which brings us to the next point.

Customize Your Resume

Each role is unique and you should customize your resume for each application. Though easier to do, submitting a generic resume may not get the attention of the Hiring Manager, especially if the requirements are very specific and the competition is very keen. A customized resume will appear more relevant and will help the resume screener have a clearer idea of whether to move you to the interview stage.

Use Keywords

You need to read through the job description very carefully to identify keywords or themes that have been mentioned and ensure that your resume highlights the very same themes. Keywords in the job description like 'strategy implementation', 'regional coverage', 'emerging markets', or 'stakeholder management' could be the main selection criteria for being called up for the interview, so ensure that these are clearly stated in your resume.

Use Multiple Entry Points

Sometimes, you can increase your chances of being noticed by the hiring manager by reaching out directly. Very often, the search process is being conducted by an HR Executive or recruiter who may not really understand your profile and dismiss your resume after the first glance. You could also ask a friend or contact in that company to make the introduction for you. This could create even more credibility if your contact is senior enough. If you can connect directly with the Hiring Manager, you would have jumped a long queue and have an immediate edge over another candidate who has only applied online.

As we are limited by the amount of time we have to conduct our job search, we need to be very focused on our activities to make sure each action we take counts for something.

Strategy #2: Be proactive, not reactive.

There is an old story about a farmer who was sitting under a tree when a large rabbit hopped by and hit its head on the trunk and died. He gleefully brought it home to his family for a feast. The next day, he decided to camp under the very same tree, waiting for another rabbit to hop by. He kept waiting under the tree for weeks whilst his field was left to ruin. Needless to say, he learnt his lesson—to survive, one has to be proactive and not reactive, naively hoping for the best to happen.

We feel that many job seekers are not being proactive enough in their job search. They sit back, visit job websites online, click the 'Apply' button and wait. And wait. And wait . . .

If you are serious about making that career switch, you need to improve your game. Here's how to be more proactive.

Are you accessing the hidden job market?

As mentioned earlier, there is a huge but hidden job market out there. Do you have access to it? How do you find it and what can you do?

Simply, by networking.

You need to stay in constant contact with your old colleagues, ex-bosses, and other industry acquaintances. Have regular discussions with them and where appropriate, let them know you are on the lookout for new roles and challenges.

As many as 80% of successful job landings occur because of a network referral.

This could be as simple as contacting a mentor or an ex-boss to let them know you are keen to explore new opportunities. Sometimes, they might be expanding their teams and may consider you for a role.

We had a client who was uncomfortable networking, and when we suggested she contact her ex-supervisor, she refused. A few months later, she was still looking for a job and we again suggested she reach out to her previous manager. This time she did. And a week later, she reported that her ex-boss had actually thought of her when he had a vacancy, but he did not contact her because he thought she was happy in her current role. He 'scolded' her for not reaching out earlier. She eventually landed the role. The moral of the story is that without initiating contact, these out-of-sight leads will never appear on your radar.

Many clients have expressed that they do not know where to start or how to network.

Networking does require some structure. Here is a suggestion. Scroll through your phone contacts and you will immediately identify individuals that you have not communicated with for a while. List the top hundred names you can immediately reconnect with. You may wish to text or reach out via a social media platform to say 'Hi, how are you doing?'. Reconnect to check in but do not immediately ask for a job lead. Share industry news, ask for insights, and stay in touch. You may even offer to help in some way—share articles, refer contacts for networking, or discuss business problems. Doing this will also demonstrate your business acumen.

Once you establish a connection, you will be at the top of their mind if a suitable opportunity arises.

From our years of career mentoring, we have observed that those who put in the most disciplined and focused effort, coupled with patience and resilience, are the ones who land their dream jobs in the shortest time. These elements are all in your control, so go ahead and be proactive today!

Understanding the 80/20 Rule

If you have an 80% chance of landing a role via active networking and only a 20% chance via job applications, why not spend 80% of your time networking instead of waiting for job alerts from job portals? Set aside 15 minutes a day to connect with people who could help you in your job search. We strongly recommend spending the majority of your effort this way as it would be a more productive use of your time.

Another interesting 80/20 rule is that 80% of your opportunities will come from 20% of your network. Networking is not just about attending events and meeting new people. It is about nurturing the networks that matter for mutual benefit.

Keep Trying

Landing the right role is a long game that takes time. Mistakes will be made and lessons will be learned, but it will rarely happen overnight. Be proactive but patient and try not to set unrealistic expectations on yourself. If you are feeling fatigued from being pro-active, give yourself a break then hop back in, but don't give up!

Strategy #3: Position yourself correctly.

We had a client who was an analyst working for a US-based market research firm and he wanted to move out of his analytics role into a business-centric one. However, he kept getting calls from headhunters for data scientist roles and was getting frustrated. We analyzed his resume and LinkedIn Profile and found that both were worded very 'quantitatively' rather than 'qualitatively'. For instance, he emphasized heavily on his statistical tools and methodology rather than on the fact he was making strategic client recommendations based on the output. As a result, he looked like a data scientist to anyone reading his profile.

We spent time tweaking his positioning and shifted the focus away from *number crunching* to *providing actionable insights*. This involved a change in mindset as well. Instead of targeting market research roles, we advised him to concentrate his efforts on consumer insights roles instead, which was the proper job title with many consumer goods companies.

Within two weeks, he started getting calls from recruiters for his targeted roles and within 3 months, he joined a global consumer healthcare company as their regional insights manager.

You will need to audit your personal brand and what others think of you when they come across your profile. Are you positioning yourself correctly or are you being misunderstood? Do recruiters know exactly what you do within ten seconds of viewing your profile?

Real Career Stories: Robert, 39, Identity Crisis Victim
Bob was a chartered accountant. He had spent a large part of his career in finance and accounting and was very good at what he did. As a valued member of his management team, he was often invited to strategy meetings and he enjoyed the nature of such work more than the usual repetitive number crunching tasks.

He then thought it would be a great idea to pivot into a commercial leadership role where he would be in charge of a department's profits and loss (P&L). He voiced his desire to his CEO who supported his idea, and he was promoted to a general manager role for a small $18 million division for him to try things out.

He performed relative well in that job and held it for 3 years. Towards the end of his stint, he realized that he did not really enjoy managing a team of 42 people and driving sales activities every day and ironically, missed his days back in finance. He was about to request for a switch back to finance and accounting when, suddenly, the company was acquired and his entire division was retrenched.

Now, he was out on the market looking for a job, and, with a baby on the way, he could not afford to be unsalaried for long. He thought it would be a great idea to apply for both general manager roles as well as finance director roles to increase his chances.

After 3 months of intensive jobhunting, he received little interest for either role. Perplexed, he spoke to us and we had to tell him the hard truth.

'Bob, your positioning is unclear. If you are applying for commercial roles, your profile just isn't robust enough as you only had 3 years with a relatively small unit which was ultimately shut down. If you are applying for finance opportunities, you have been effectively out of that for over 3 years and there will be doubts as to whether you can step back into those shoes again. You will need to select one positioning and craft your branding and narrative to reinforce it. Having a confusing profile like yours makes headhunters not want to consider you for either role.'

Here are some quick tips on developing your positioning and branding.

Understand Your Talent Market

What is the current situation in your market? Is it very saturated with job applicants who have very similar profiles? What skills are employers currently seeking, and which skills are scarce in the market? You need to understand the demand-side dynamics of the talent market and adjust your pitch accordingly. If there is a growing demand for a particular skill that you do not have, you might want to consider getting trained in it, such as data analytics, digital marketing, etc. Once you have a thorough understanding of the skills-demand landscape, you can craft your message to fit that demand.

What do you want to be known for?

In the noisy and crowded talent market, how would you stand out? Are you the person who 'sells machines' or are you the 'regional leader who specializes in growing sales of precision machinery in emerging markets'?

Look towards your core skills and abilities to make your pitch unique.

Ask a Professional

One of the quickest ways to build your positioning is to engage a professional coach to review your current brand. Getting a friend or colleague who already knows you can only get you so far because they already have a preconceived notion of what you are. Moreover, they may not be from your industry or be as skilled in crafting your branding and positioning as a trained professional, so the investment will be well worth it.

We would strongly advise you to audit and review your current brand and see if it is congruent with the career direction and strategy. This is even more critical if you are deciding on a career switch into something radically different and need to reinvent yourself.

Strategy #4 — Interview strategically

Understanding your unique selling proposition will help you position yourself better in your job search. Thinking strategically about the interviewer's challenges, the company's problems, and how you can resolve them will ensure you make a powerful impact during the interview. It's not enough to emphasize that you fit the requirements of the role. You must express what you can do to help the company make more revenue, save costs, be more efficient, solve problems, and most importantly, support the business leaders in their quest to meet their targets.

Research and Preparation for the Interview

The most important aspect of interview preparation is research. You should research the company extensively: the products, the people, the business strategies, the competitors, their customers, and more. Visit the company's corporate website, check their annual reports and scan the news. Use LinkedIn to view the profiles of the interviewers and see whether you might have any contacts in common. From this research, you can develop questions to get more clarity on their expectations of you and the role. Having done some research, you can now reach out to your network to get more information on current issues and significant industry developments.

Besides preparing for the questions, it is also important that you prepare yourself mentally. If you're feeling anxious, try to think of the interview as just another meeting. You have attended plenty of meetings in your lifetime. This is just another meeting where you focus on trying to help a hiring manager. There is really no need to feel nervous as the interviewer is probably hoping you will be a strong candidate. Remember that you are just there to see if you can help.

Know what Interviewers Look for

Interviewers are usually assessing you on three major areas: your **ability**, **motivation**, and whether you will **fit** in with the organization, its culture, and practices.

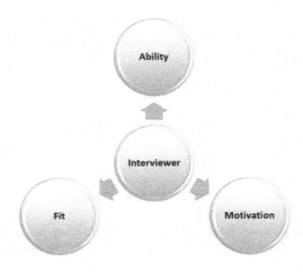

When they assess your **ability**, they are assessing whether you can do the job. They may reference a specific achievement listed in your resume and ask you for more information. They might ask you specific questions around competencies or tasks like, 'Tell me about a specific project you're proud of' or 'Have you ever had to design and execute a marketing program from scratch?'.

For **motivation**, they are assessing your level of interest or willingness to work in the organization. They might ask questions like, 'What interests you about the company?', 'Why did you choose to build a career in this industry?', or 'Why are you looking for a job change?'.

And for the **fit**, they want to know if you are able to integrate seamlessly into their working environment or culture. These questions can be wide ranging as they ask you about issues that are important to them. They might ask, 'What is your opinion on working overtime?' or 'Tell me about a particularly challenging customer you've had to manage,' or 'Have you worked with difficult people? Please describe them and how you managed them.'

If you can assure them that you have the **ability** to do the job well, the **motivation** to join their team, and will be a good **fit** for the culture, your chances of landing the role have improved tremendously.

Have a Strong Introduction

It is true that the first 15 seconds are the most important when forming a first impression. That is why you should prepare a powerful introduction. It doesn't matter if the interviewer starts off with 'Tell Me about yourself' or 'What brings you here?'. At the early stages of the interview, you should introduce yourself and share your background.

Most candidates have a tendency to over-elaborate during their introduction and go into too much detail, only to trail off, not knowing how to conclude. A strong introduction for an interview goes straight to your key selling points and concludes with a positive statement of interest in the role and how you can add value to their business.

Here are some examples of a strong introduction:

- 'Thank you for your time today. As you can see from my resume, I've had 12 years of consulting experience, and I specialize in HR analytics. I've done project A and worked on project B. I'm really excited to understand a little more about your current setup and how I can help.'
- 'Thank you for your time today. When John referred me to you, he highlighted that you needed someone to manage the entire supply chain operations. I've had 15 years' of experience in managing the entire value chain for Company ABC, and most recently, I've been involved in Project X, where I've had to completely revamp the system. I'm really happy to finally meet with you to find out more about your situation and what your plans are.'

Always conclude your introduction with a strong statement of interest or value-add.

Real Career Stories: Vera, 45, Logistics Manager

I hated interviews. They made me very uncomfortable, especially the way the interviewers behave when they ask you all those difficult questions and how they gave those judgmental looks when you don't answer those questions correctly or to their satisfaction. I could never overcome that sense of nervousness during interviews, that's why I've always had difficulty landing jobs.

Then, one day, I overheard my HR colleague getting yelled at by her boss for not being able to fill a particularly difficult role. She said that she had interviewed 9 candidates hoping one would work out, but none of them did. She was desperate to fill the role and was under tremendous pressure.

It was only then that I realized that often the interviewers were just as stressed as the interviewees, and the questions they asked were more to qualify the candidate rather than disqualify them from the role.

My mindset changed and I suddenly didn't feel so stressed during interviews again. In fact, as much as they were choosing me, I was also choosing them and if I wasn't comfortable with any term or condition, I could decline their offer. The power wasn't only in their hands, it was in mine too, so I shouldn't really feel too nervous at all.

Respond with Good Answers

You will be asked many questions during the interview. Is there a structured technique for answering all these questions?

Yes, there is.

Use the **STAR** technique when answering competency questions.

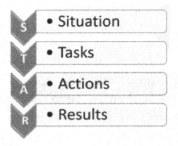

STAR stands for Situation, Tasks, Actions, and Results. Focus on results and outcomes, then conclude with how you can contribute. For example, the interviewer might ask, 'Tell us about a complex project you've had to handle'.

You may answer, 'Most recently, I worked on XYZ project *[Situation]*, leading an extended team of 200 executives *[Task]* rolling out the solution across 15 cities *[Action]*, and I'm happy to report that we're due to complete the final phase this quarter *[Result]*. In my career, I've worked on multiple large scale infrastructure projects across the region *[Situation]*, and managed not just our own internal teams, but every external stakeholder there is—the vendors, the business partners, and the government agencies *[Action]*. I understand the dynamics of complicated relationships, and am able to influence decisions. As a result, I have consistently met my deadlines. *[Result]*'

Some candidates report that they hate being asked about their strengths and weaknesses. If you're asked about what your strengths are, focus on the key skills required for the job. Validate with examples and conclude with how you can contribute.

For example, 'My previous bosses and all my performance reviews have highlighted that I am really good at analyzing data, especially for the FMCG industry. I can take a complex set of data, map that against what the business units want to find out, leverage previous research, and generate useful insights, trends, and patterns. Having been in this industry now for over 5 years, I know what questions to ask and can make useful recommendations'.

Sometimes, the questions asked during the interview can be tricky. One common one is, 'What is your weakness?'. Focus on area for improvement like this: 'I constantly seek self-improvement. One area I'm currently working on to improve is how to manage teams that are geographically separated. I've got a couple of mentors who give me regular advice, and I see this as a continuous improvement effort on my part'.

Occasionally we get unusual questions. We might be asked about our ambitions, favourite book, superpower, or what we do with our spare time. Stay authentic. Don't give cliché answers. Just in case, always have a go-to author or book that is interesting and insightful that you can discuss.

Answer Salary Questions Confidently

During the interview, you may sometimes be asked about your salary expectations. Do your research and be prepared to answer the question in a matter-of-fact tone, expressing your knowledge of the market rates, and be ready to share your expectations.

Provide a range that you are comfortable with, saying something like, 'My salary expectation for this job scope is in the region of $120,000 to $140,000 per year'.

You might even be asked about your current compensation. If you are uncomfortable revealing the details, you may choose to keep this information confidential or provide a ballpark figure. You can respond with, 'I'm not too comfortable sharing my *exact* compensation with you, but for benchmarking purposes, it is in the region of $200,000 per year with extra benefits and allowances'.

We know that salary discussions can be a bit stressful and uncomfortable, so you should know your numbers and be prepared to answer as smoothly as possible.

Power Tip from the Authors

As a headhunter, one of our pet peeves is when the candidate we speak with refuses to give us information regarding their salary when we ask—not even an indicative ball-park figure.

We would get responses like, 'Why would you want to know?', 'What I'm paid has no relevance to any job you're going to offer me,' and 'If I tell you my current salary, you will use it to depress my future salary, so I'm not going to tell you.'

Now, we understand that revealing such sensitive information may have its inherent risks, but the reason why we ask this question is not to judge you, rather, it is to find out whether the role is going to be worth your time exploring.

For instance, we could be approaching you for a role that's either too junior or too senior for you. So, by getting a rough gauge of your salary range, we will be able to estimate if this would be at the right level for you.

From personal experience, the candidates who put up the most resistance to offering this information are usually the ones with their own salary issues. They either feel too lowly paid and want a huge salary jump, or are too senior and are currently looking to downshift.

Both these reasons are legitimate, but if you are giving the recruiter so much aggravation at the start of the process, there is a high chance that salary negotiations will be even more painful at the acceptance stage when there is an actual offer in your hand.

Experienced headhunters steer clear of these 'salary aggressive' individuals and move their attention quickly onto other candidates who seem easier to manage. Please remain professional and helpful.

Prepare Questions for the Interviewer

An interview should never be a one-sided conversation but a two-way career discussion. As you are doing your research, you will probably develop several questions about the role, the scope, and the challenges. Examples might include how a specific market is performing or who they perceive as their biggest competitor and why.

You do not have to reserve your questions for the end of the interview and it is perfectly acceptable for you to ask any relevant questions during the discussion itself.

What are some good questions to ask during the interview?

Do not just ask basic questions like the expectations of the role, how you will be measured, the company's culture, or the hiring manager's leadership style. A very impactful question you can ask is 'What is your most immediate challenge that the successful candidate can help you out with?'

Listen closely to the answer, then respond with three ways in which you can be of immediate help to solving their challenge. It is a great opportunity to reinforce your capabilities with the interviewer.

Real Career Stories: Neil, 42, Technology Director

Neil was very surprised when the CEO of the one of the country's leading start-ups called him up personally to arrange for a job interview. He seemed very personable and friendly and invited Neil to his office for an official interview—on a Sunday at 3.00 p.m. in the afternoon.

It seemed like a strange timing for Neil as it was unusual to have such meetings on a weekend at the office but he obliged anyway. Neil arrived at the office and, to his surprise, he saw that it was full of employees. Everyone there was working as though it was a normal workday, going about their usual buzz.

The receptionist brought him to the CEO's office and they began the interview. It went very well for an hour and the CEO stopped and smugly said, 'In this office, we work very hard. We don't believe in work-life balance. Seventy-hour work weeks are normal here because there's so much to do. So, if you aren't prepared to put in those hours, this is probably not the place for you. We don't hire wimps here'.

Neil smiled and said, 'Thanks for sharing, but I'm afraid work-life balance is rather important to me as I do not believe this pace is sustainable. I appreciate your time, but I don't think this is going to work out'. Neil then excused himself and walked out.

'Sometimes, the interview is a great opportunity to "sample" the boss and the work environment. I could not subscribe to the CEO's values and was not willing to sacrifice my personal and family life to benefit his business. I'm glad he gave me an inside view and am actually grateful that I was learning all this before I joined.'

Eight months later, the company shut down because of poor customer service due to excessive employee turnover.

Ending the Interview

At the end of the interview, there is one very important question you will need to ask. This question is the 'next step' question, and it goes like this. 'What would be the next step for me and when can I expect to hear from you again?'

The answer to this question can sometimes tell you if you have done well for the interview and whether you will be expecting to progress to the next stage.

Get a sense of timing and whether it's okay for you to follow up at an agreed point in the future. When the meeting is over, always send a 'thank you' note and be sure to follow up as promised.

Interviews are Not Scary

Organizations are looking to hire the best person to fill the position. The interviewers are busy managers and have performance metrics to meet. Your job is to help them fulfill their corporate targets. Focus on your ability to contribute to the team and help the manager meet his goals. Interviews don't have to be nerve-racking. So, prepare well and get as much practice as possible, and you will be strong in your delivery.

Strategy #5: Don't depend on recruiters

An angry candidate once shouted at his recruiter, *'What kind of a headhunter are you? You haven't even found me a job yet!'*

Clearly, there are many in the market who still don't quite understand what headhunters and recruiters do. Let us explain here. You must understand that the primary role of search professionals is very clear. They are paid to find the right candidate for their paying client hence they do not work for you! Do not expect the headhunter to go out into the market with your resume in hand, knocking on doors, pitching your profile to every client they meet, or to give you regular updates on how much progress they've had in promoting you in the market. You would be very surprised at the number of people we have met who simply park their resumes with the recruiters and expect magic to happen. This method is far too passive and it surrenders all your power to them.

If you do meet one who is open to using your profile to go to market, do note that you have no control over who they meet, and therefore who is seeing your confidential resume. Also note that once they open a door to an opportunity that fits you, yours will certainly not be the only profile they submit.

How to Work With Recruiters

Be Specific

If you are planning to enlist the help of recruiters, by all means, go ahead! Many are very friendly and approachable. However, do be very specific.

Recruiters usually have specialized industries that they focus on, for instance, healthcare, banking, or energy. Some may specialize according to functions like finance, marketing, or technology. So, do your homework and make sure you are not wasting anyone's time.

Once you have determined the right one to approach, be very specific with the type of roles you are interested in. This will give them a clearer idea on what to do with you and help jolt their imagination when they meet their clients.

Be Helpful

Always be prepared with your elevator pitch. Listen to what they have to say, and even if it isn't the right role for you, do not waste a good opportunity to build powerful networks. Refer friends who might be relevant to them and offer as much help as possible. By being helpful and friendly, they will remember you when a suitable opportunity comes along.

Don't be Pushy

A recruiter receives an average of fifty unsolicited resumes a day. If you are sending your resume in such a fashion, it is all right to follow up with a courtesy call. However, do not stalk them every day, reminding them to look for jobs for you. Most of them are under a lot of pressure from their clients and bosses to close their deals and would not appreciate any additional stress from their candidates.

Keep in Contact

Remember to stay in contact with your recruiter. A short email or call would suffice. Stay on their radar so that when the right opportunity comes along, they will recall your profile. We suggest a monthly email to briefly say 'hello' and update them on any changes on your side, or you could even share some interesting market news which would be very welcome. Treat Recruiters like a 'marketing channel' for your job search, but not your only channel. If utilized properly, they can be a very effective means of increasing your reach and accessing opportunities, but do not depend too heavily on them in your job search.

Strategy #6 - Leverage the Power Of LinkedIn

A mentor once joked, 'How are you expecting to win the million-dollar lottery when you haven't even bought a ticket?' Likewise, how are you hoping to land a dream role if you are not even present on LinkedIn, the world's largest professional online network, when all hiring managers, recruiters and HR leaders are using it to search for fresh talents?

Why LinkedIn is Important

LinkedIn is currently the biggest professional networking platform in the world with more than half a billion members. Almost all decision-makers in the hiring chain will use LinkedIn either to search for candidates or check profiles to learn more about the job applicant's history. In fact, LinkedIn is one of the biggest disruptors of the recruitment industry globally and many recruitment agencies have been displaced by them. So, it is critical that you have a presence on this valuable platform, and more importantly, are using it correctly.

How is Your Visibility?

We will assume you already have a LinkedIn account. How many people are you currently connected with? LinkedIn works on the basis of connections, so the more connections you have, the wider your network becomes. We recommend a minimum of 500 contacts if you are a new user on this platform. Some LinkedIn experts feel that 2,000 would be an ideal number of contacts for optimal visibility. For a start, you can quickly ramp up your connections by seeking out old colleagues, classmates, and friends to connect with. You can expand this further by connecting to fellow professionals in your field or even to colleagues in your company.

What is your message?

When people land on your LinkedIn page, what is the first thing that comes to mind? Are they able to get a clear sense of what exactly you do or do they need to scroll further just to figure out your competencies and experiences? Your messaging needs to be very clear at the 'above the fold' level. This is a term advertisers used to describe newspaper headlines and mastheads, i.e., the most visible part of the front page of the newspapers. You need to position yourself so clearly that recruiters can pinpoint exactly which industry you are in and what specific role you play.

This can be achieved by clear wording in your headline and a strong and emotive banner image. Your summary needs to be concise, providing enough context and scope for the reader to digest at one glance. You do not want the prospective hiring manager to leave your page after 15 seconds of fruitlessly trying to figure out what you are. That would be a waste of opportunity indeed.

Be Active

LinkedIn rewards active users with better visibility. Members with an 'All-Star' rating are up to 40 times more likely to be contacted by a recruiter. You can also increase your chances by being active on LinkedIn. Posting and sharing interesting stories or writing articles will increase your engagement scores and raise your brand on the platform. This in turn creates awareness and reinforces your positioning in the market, especially when you post industry-relevant content. For example, if you want to strengthen your brand as an insurance industry expert, posting the latest news along with your professional and unique point of view will give others the impression that you are being a thought leader in this space.

Even simple actions can have a positive effect on your engagement scores. 'Liking', 'Commenting', and 'Sharing' posts by others will put you on their radar and increase their likelihood of looking at your profile to find out more about you. This is particularly effective for getting on your target's radar.

Real Career Stories: Ben, 51, HR Consultant

Ben was an HR consultant who never felt the need for updating himself with technology and social media. However, he attended a talk by a self-professed LinkedIn guru who told him, 'Any publicity on LinkedIn is good publicity. Just put your name out there in the market and the recruiters will start calling. Make at least one post a day. Kitten videos get the most likes and comments'.

So, Ben started posting materials on a daily basis. When he ran out of good materials to share, he posted 'dad jokes' like 'What do you call a fish wearing a bowtie? SoFishticated.' He also posted his thoughts about controversial issues of the day like politics where he made some very strong comments.

He had been applying for several jobs at various HR consultancy firms but unsurprisingly, he never got past the first interview. Out of frustration, he asked his headhunter friend why this was so, and he was told, 'The fact is, your regular postings on LinkedIn have branded you as a "reputational risk" to many organizations. You are supposed to be an expert in HR matters but your "dad jokes" are making you look rather unprofessional and is taking away your credibility'.

From that day onwards, Ben stopped all his frivolous posts on LinkedIn and started to take his public image more seriously. He learnt an important lesson that social media was a powerful tool that could cut both ways and that he had to be careful with his posts.

Use LinkedIn as a Connecting Tool

Because almost 95% of executives and decision makers are already on LinkedIn, there lies a treasure trove of prospective targets you can connect with. Get on their radar by sending them a customized invite and if you have curated your branding and messaging on your profile page correctly, they will be intrigued by what you could potentially do for them and might even reach out to you. Over time, you would have a very robust network of like-minded professionals in the market.

Like it or not, LinkedIn is here to stay. It is as ubiquitous as the mobile phone and if used correctly, can be one of the most powerful tools in your job search arsenal.

Strategy #7: Take control of your campaign

The job-seeking process can pull you in all sorts of directions. At any given point, you have to juggle many activities—a meeting with an ex-colleague, a coffee with a recruiter, follow up emails to write, LinkedIn posts, corporate websites to research, phone calls to make, interviews to prepare for, and a host of other to-do items. Planning your job search campaign can minimize frustrations and help you stay on top of your game.

Keep a Planner or Record of Your Campaign

Some candidates we have met prefer excel spreadsheets to:

- log each job opportunity with all the details: application date, interviews, remarks, and follow up plans.
- log every meeting with every recruiter with personal notes on the meeting and follow up actions.
- make a list of every person they met or contacted, details of information shared, and follow up plans.

- build a target list of every company they want to work for, which helps with research and penetration strategies.

Other candidates have used mind maps to have a big picture of their target market and corresponding follow up items. Mind maps are very effective visual reminders of what needs to be done.

Write an Action Plan for the Week or the Month

Because you could be easily distracted by your day job and not concentrate on what is really needed for the job search, having a written action plan will allow you to list down and take charge of what needs to be done. Having an action plan allows you to focus and prioritize key activities like networking, job applications, and important calls to make. If you want to succeed in landing a new job, you have to undertake the job search effort seriously. Treat it like you would any other important project at work. Allocate time, energy, and resources and maintain discipline in keeping track of the process.

Part G

Common Career Questions

13

Common Career Questions

Over the years, we have encountered hundreds of burning career questions and interestingly, many of them are quite similar. These questions plague a large number of executives at different points in their careers and we would like to address some of the more common ones here.

Q1. I'm not sure about my future. What's next?

From our experience coaching the thousands of mid-career crossroaders, they typically start with 'I don't know what to do next'. After some probing, most of them do know what they want, but are intimidated by the obstacles and the effort required. With some coaching and Career Strategy development (see Chapters 5 and 6), they often overcome their perceived constraints and move on in their career trajectory. Career changes are scary and it's comforting to know you have someone in your corner who's rooting for you and has no other agenda.

For those who truly don't know what they want to do, reviewing all the variables described in this book will give them clear clues to follow. From there, market research and networking activities should surface opportunities. The journey may not be a simple one, but with some guidance, a clear strategy and a roadmap, they get there in the end. Typical career switches can take anywhere from 3 months to a year. Please also refer to the chapter on crossover quadrants and pivots (Chapter 7).

Sometimes the 'I don't know what to do' stems from their fears of commitment, failure, and the unknown. It's normal to say, 'I just want to be offered a job, any job'.

We have the same advice—review all the career variables described in this book, speak to your mentors, get a career coach, define your goals, then strategize the activities required to meet those goals. Set a timeline and make decisions at each step.

Q2. What if I tried to make a career move and fail?

We get this objection frequently. While nobody can provide absolute certainties, having a smart Career Strategy will improve your chances of success. However, the bigger question to ask is, 'What if I don't try?' Will you be stuck in the same role, feeling frustrated going to work every day for the rest of your life? Will you become obsolete and irrelevant to the job market? Often, the status quo is just as risky as making a move, so don't be afraid of trying something different.

You could potentially mitigate your risk by creating a backup plan or two. Conventional wisdom says if you fail to plan, you plan to fail. You can easily reduce your risk by partnering with a good Career Strategist who can give you an objective opinion and good advice to guide you through any self-doubt to validate your plans, play the devil's advocate, and crystalize your game plan each step of the way.

Q3. Do you have an example of somebody who successfully pivoted into a different career?

We recently had a senior global sales leader who decided she wanted to pivot to sales training. This was something she wanted to do for a long time, but salary-wise, the sales role was more lucrative and she was good at it. The sales commissions were simply too attractive and she stayed on for 20 years. However, in early 2020, Covid-19 happened and she was retrenched as the company pulled out of the market. With nothing to lose, she decided to try making the switch to Training. In partnership with her career coach, she gave herself a timeline of 6 months to pursue her interests. She networked with trainers from various industries, signed up for a professional training course to learn the fundamentals, and certified with a sales training program provider to be able to train using their proprietary content. She also picked up multiple pro-bono speaking and training engagements to increase her visibility and gain experience. Her previous employer has since invited her back to conduct regional training sessions for a professional fee.

She managed to find a regional training manager role which was 2 levels below her previous one, but it didn't matter to her as she just wanted to get a foothold into this new vocation. Analyzing and planning training needs across the region was fairly straightforward for her given her previous experience as a sales leader, but most importantly, she enjoyed it tremendously. She shared with us that she is happier now as she has more autonomy over her work. She plans to widen her training scope to include academic institutions and organizations in her previous industry.

Q4. Help! I've Been Retrenched. What Should I Do?

Given today's volatile economy, retrenchments have become the norm. It is impossible to control all the external forces, and, occasionally, bad things do happen. If your company was acquired, expect changes, even if the acquiring entity says they will maintain the status quo . . . *for now.*

Being the agile executive that you are, when a significant event takes place or is about to happen, you should immediately mobilize your network to look at alternatives. You can attempt to build relationships with your new managers or disembark from this ship to find another. Pay attention to any rumours of an upcoming downsizing. As the saying goes, there is no smoke without fire.

The Career Pandas, who can sometimes be blissfully ignorant, are often the ones who get caught off guard and usually cry foul that they did not see it coming.

Sometimes, we meet people who are in denial, saying things like 'It will never happen to me'.

No matter how mentally prepared you are, you will still experience some degree of shock when it happens. Many people report a grieving cycle of shock, anger, denial, bargaining, and acceptance, sometimes multiple times in the same day.

Take a day or two to come to terms and to formulate immediate plans. If you have been provided an outplacement support service, take it up. At the very least, you will have someone to help you with your job search strategies and to get your job search tools ready. Also, leverage any employment assistance plans or union support.

Speak to the professionals to ensure that you have received a fair severance and due process since regulations, protocols and policies on employee exits differ with every company, industry, and country.

Emotionally, it's hard to have any clarity of thought to make and execute plans if you're distressed. Seek professional help, speak to loved ones, exercise, and do whatever it takes to help you get some mental clarity for your next steps.

Q5: What else should I do after being retrenched?

If you have started your job search activities, keep progressing any opportunities you already have in your pipeline, amplify networking efforts, and expedite meetings to surface more leads. At the same time, you could try to negotiate for a longer garden leave or notice period so that you have some buffer to manage your affairs, such as ensuring a smooth transition of your tasks and responsibilities and updating your stakeholders (both internal and external) to ensure they know who to go to. You might also want to do your medical check-ups too.

Plan your exit story well.

There are some individuals who are very uncomfortable revealing to their network or future employer that they were retrenched. Let us assure you that because of the widespread nature of retrenchments, being exited is no longer an issue; in fact, some employers prefer the fact that you can start work sooner.

Simply share with your future employer that you were retrenched as a part of a larger corporate restructuring initiative. Emphasize that you completely understand the business rationale, and if you were in charge, you'd probably make the same call. Be positive, show enthusiasm for the future and give the interviewers confidence that you are ready for the next chapter of your career!

Q6: How do I help a friend who has been retrenched?

Companies are constantly restructuring and retrenchments are common. Impacted employees may not be able to find new roles quickly, which can be depressing. How, then, can you support a friend who has just been retrenched?

Here are 3 ideas.

Be encouraging, not condescending.

There's a difference between 'I know how you feel, I've been there before . . . but I found a job in 1 month' and 'I can't imagine how hard this must be for you, but I'm sure things will improve'.

Remember, when you're helping a friend in this state, it's not about you. It's about them.

Encourage them to think of the past where they overcame a similarly tough situation. Be supportive, provide a listening ear and tell them things are going to be alright.

Be practical.

Someone who just lost his job doesn't need your 'thoughts and prayers', or your condolences and pity. What they need are solid job leads or just good advice. If you're in the same industry or have similar job functions, do pass on leads to them. You might even want to give them contacts of recruiters whom you have spoken to before. Offer to connect them to your network and be their advocate. Speak to your networks about them to see if there are any suitable vacancies.

Be there.

Check in on them regularly. Even a simple text message would cheer them up. Ask if they need anything. As long as you let them know you are available to talk when they are ready, they will come to you once they feel the time is right.

It's never easy being retrenched and having good and supportive friends around you helps a lot.

Q7. I have been working at my company for 18 years and was offered a choice between a retrenchment package and a transfer to another department. Which one should I choose?

Eighteen years is a long time, and hopefully, there is a generous retrenchment package involved. Instead of being too troubled, some would look upon this as a 'happy problem' but a problem nonetheless. On one hand, you will have a nice windfall if you choose to exit. But on the other, you have an option to extend your career. How nice if you could have your cake and eat it, too! But the harsh reality is that you probably can't do both, so let's look at both options closely.

If you exit . . .

You will probably get to enjoy a short career break to recharge for your next move. With that sizable bonus sitting in your bank, you could even take the much-needed sabbatical you've always dreamed of.

However, there is always a limit to how much resting and relaxing you can enjoy before (a) you get bored, (b) your spouse gets annoyed by your constant presence at home, and/or (c) you run out of money. Ultimately, you will probably need to find a new job.

How confident are you in your skillsets and abilities that you know you'll find a role quickly?

If you know you can command a similar role at the same level in another company (your present organization's competitor, perhaps?) and they would love to hire you, then by all means, as Steve Miller Band puts it,' Take the money and run!' and accept the golden handshake.

If you are not confident of landing a job with your current skillsets and experience, then you could re-skill yourself and take up a course in a new or related field. Take this break to design the next phase of your career. If you need help, engage a career coach for advice.

If you stay . . .

If you forego that nice package and take up the new role, you could probably face a significant degree of uncertainty as well. Will the new role suit you? Is it something you'll enjoy doing? Is the new boss to your liking? How stable is that role?

Sure, you may bask in the nice and warm feeling of job security for the first few months, but as reality sets in, you may come to see that the new role may not offer you any more security that the last one you had. Besides, is there any job security these days, anyway?

We have seen cases where candidates turned down redundancy packages out of fear or loyalty, only to take on a new role and hate it so much that they resigned 6 months later with nothing in hand. Ultimately, there is no right or wrong answer here and the last place to get answers to important life-questions is the Internet.

Our advice is to take your time to think about it and speak to your career coach or mentors about this. They will be able to provide some clarity around it.

Q8. Is it okay to take a career break?

The short answer is yes. Many individuals have taken long career breaks and re-entered the job market successfully. Many retrenched staff take time off to recharge and plan their next moves and may even have the luxury of a longer break as they may have received a generous pay-out.

There are various reasons for taking a career break. If your health has been impacted by your job, this can make a huge difference in terms of recuperating and recharging yourself. You can return to the workforce refreshed and productive. Some individuals even take months off to coach their children during critical examinations or to look after elderly parents who may need caregiver support.

Career breaks are no longer taboo and if you feel you need one and can afford one, do not be afraid to consider it.

Q9. I've been on a career break. How do I tell my interviewer about this?

As mentioned earlier, there is little stigma associated with career breaks in this age of volatility and uncertainty. What is more important than the break itself is what you were doing during that time. If you had spent the 6 months enriching yourself with the latest data analytics course or digital marketing program, it would be a great example of how you had invested your time wisely.

However, if you spent the entire period binge watching every series on Netflix, then questions will arise as to what value the career break added to your life. It is important to take a break from work for as long as you need the space to recuperate physically from illness, mentally from work fatigue, or emotionally from a toxic workplace. However, it would still be wise to be seen as having improved yourself during that period in some way, shape, or form. So, sign up for courses to update yourself.

If you are asked by your interviewer, be forthcoming and respond, 'After I left my previous job, I took a short career break to recharge and refocus my energy on the next role ahead. I took up courses in data analytics, conducted some consulting work with my clients, and helped build a library for an orphanage in Cambodia'.

Do not apologize for your sabbatical or career break but demonstrate how that period has enriched you in ways that can benefit your new employers.

Q10. I hate my job! What can I do?

It is important to know what the actual reasons are and when you started feeling this way.

What was the trigger? Who was the trigger? Is this trigger cyclical, permanent, or temporary?

For instance, a client wanted to quit her job because of intense work pressure. It all started when her company acquired a competitor and her team and responsibilities doubled overnight. The additional work was tiring her out, but she realized that it was only temporary as the company was going to merge the department with another business unit and she was only acting as a 'temporary custodian' in the interim.

What aspects of your work do you hate the most? Is it an emotional response to a transient occurrence or is there a systemic issue that is slowly draining your energies? Break your role down into individual tasks and responsibilities. Make a list and conduct an objective audit. Identify which parts of your job you enjoy and which parts that is causing you unnecessary stress. Speak to your leaders about how you can be more effective at your work and explore options of job redesign with them.

Q11. I hate my boss! What can I do?

Once again, let us start with 'why?'.

How long have you had to report to this boss and what behaviours have you noticed that led to your feelings of dislike? Is it mistrust? Is your belief that there might be something suspicious going on, based on fact or just a feeling?

Reframe the issue and put yourself in your boss' shoes. What are his or her KPIs? Where is the pressure coming from? As a team member, are you a hindrance or are you a valued asset? Have you been consistent in aligning your professional objectives with your boss' or have you been adversarial? Or is it based on mismatched values? Review Chapter 9 on self-assessment and figure out what your values are, and then try and make an educated guess as to your boss' values. True values are observed, not articulated. Your boss' actions and decisions are clues to his or her values. Do your values align?

We have spoken about aligning your values to your company as well as to your leaders. Being aware of what drives your leaders means you can be more calculated and careful with your work, avoiding missteps that can damage your relationships.

However, if you do have a boss who is unreasonable, toxic or overtly disrespectful, you have 3 options you might want to consider.

The first is to find ways to be able to work with him or her.

Have an 'adult conversation' to highlight what is working and what isn't. No relationship is perfect and you might have to learn to tolerate behaviours until a point where you find it unacceptable. Then, try this second option, which is to find another boss, internally or externally.

Lobby your way into another department or network externally to see if there are other opportunities available. Speak with colleagues in other departments to find out whether they are hiring and if they might consider bringing you onboard. You might also want to speak to recruiters to see if there are other external opportunities you could explore.

Finally, you could try outlasting your boss.

If you do not wish to leave your company or department, you might want to play the waiting game and see if you can outlast this terrible leader. Many managers have succeeded in getting themselves fired from the company because of questionable behaviour. Yours might be one of those, so be patient.

Q12. My colleagues are toxic. What can I do?

Start documenting the toxic behaviours. Note the details including the people involved, the date, time, and where it happened. Be a journalist and start collecting evidence of bad behaviours because memories fade and perspectives change. Without proof and documentation, it will be difficult to look for a pattern.

The purpose of this is to see if you are reacting to mere casual incidents or if there is a real cause for concern. Distinguish between what is real and actual versus your emotional response just because these are people you might not like.

Work with your mentor or coach to figure out strategies to manage the people around you. Is there something you can do to improve your relationship with your colleagues? Are there others who have similar problems with these so-called toxic individuals?

Are they really toxic or is there something else going on? This might be harsh, but do consider your part as well—could you be the problem?

Take the time to hone your influencing and persuasion skills. Actively seek a way to improve your relationships, to lobby the leadership for policies that increase harmony and team-bonding, and ask HR to initiate compensation policies that encourage teamwork rather than competition.

Do not quit your job impulsively because of a few negative people. Make strategic decisions with a clear mind. Seek greener pastures that are aligned with your overall Career Strategy. The truth is that all jobs have their ups and downs and every environment has its share of unpleasant characters. Your strategy is to rise above it and to focus on doing a good job and accelerating your career, leaving all the haters behind.

Q13. Help me, I've lost my Sponsor.

We have discussed in previous chapters how sponsors can help facilitate your career. Having a Sponsor is a powerful strategy to getting promoted or being offered growth opportunities. Some of our senior level clients have reached their positions with the support of Sponsors higher up the chain of command. But when they suddenly lose their Sponsors, their careers can get bumpy.

When you lose your Sponsor, you might not have the support to pitch for a promotion, a high-profile project, or any initiatives of your choosing. Worse still, some executives become vulnerable to corporate restructuring without the protection of their sponsors and may find their jobs suddenly at risk.

So, what can you do?

Find another Sponsor.

In any large corporate environment, it's important to widen your strategic network. Look for other senior leaders whom you can look up to and work towards making yourself part of their inner circle. This will require a lot of networking and trust building and might take some time. Be patient because this will be worth the effort.

Get your sponsor to bring you along.

Sponsors who move on to other organizations in other roles will usually take their protégés with them. If your Sponsor is making such a move, ask if you can join the new endeavour. It could even be a great career opportunity.

Make a new pivot.

If your Sponsor is gone, you could align yourself to your new leaders. Proactively approach them and show them that you are a valuable asset to the company. Ask them how you can help them achieve their goals and start supporting them as soon as you can.

Get ready to leave.

Your last resort is to consider exiting the business unit or even the company. Start developing your job search strategy and commence the job hunting process.

Q14. I don't know how to network.

Humans are social creatures and as long as you are genuine about building a meaningful two-way relationship, you're networking. It is not that difficult.

Begin with warm leads and contacts. Reach out to old friends, ex-colleagues, and even former bosses or classmates. Your business contacts like your suppliers, vendors, and clients could be a good starting point for your networking activities as well. The biggest point to note is that networking is not about just meeting strangers and connecting on LinkedIn. True networking is about consistent connections and conversations. It's an ongoing professional and sometimes personal relationship where you help each other.

Be proactive. If you expect others to initiate contact, you're limiting yourself. Actively reach out to colleagues from other departments. Attempt to have lunch or drinks with an industry contact weekly or at least once a month. Join professional associations and get involved in their events. Volunteer your time and you will have the opportunities to build relationships and shared experiences with fellow industry professionals.

Q15. I think I'm not landing a job because I'm too old.

'I've applied for more than 20 jobs, and I did not hear back from a single one. They probably think I'm too old for the job.'

If you are in your late 40s or 50s, these statements might sound familiar during your job search. Let's be real. Sometimes, it *is* about age. If you're in a role where your age could be a negative factor, like basic computer programming, then it could be difficult for the employer to justify hiring you when he can get a younger and cheaper individual to do the same tasks.

But there are roles where age is an advantage. Most leadership positions favour seniority and experience. They value key skills like managing stakeholders, influencing and pulling teams together, and the ability to leverage connections and networks to get initiatives off the ground. Employers would love to hire an experienced individual who can immediately hit the ground running based on deep domain experience.

We have coached individuals over 60 who project the image and energy of 40-year olds. We have also met 50-year-old individuals who talk like they're 85! Age is a social construct.

One 67-year-old client was an amazingly positive individual with high energy levels. Although he was actively looking for roles, he did not indicate in any way that he was desperate for one. He continued to share his expertise, readily helping his ex-colleagues, his industry network, and anyone who asked. He enjoyed meeting people and was generous in sharing his knowledge. As he networked, it became apparent that he was the subject matter expert and subsequently received a job offer with a competitive salary.

If you feel that you are being unfairly discriminated against because of your age, you might want to focus on the relevant skills and experience that you can offer instead. If you can't articulate your skills or differentiate yourself, there would be no reason to hire you.

Review all your years of experience. What skills do you have? Who are the people you've worked with? What are you known for? Build a list of competencies, knowledge, and skills that, when combined, makes you an irresistible package to support your future employers in their vision.

We have helped many people to uncover their unique value proposition. Sometimes, it is a matter of seeing how much they have accomplished. Many individuals have expressed that they've forgotten, or they have simply been taking their skills for granted.

Move away from an 'It's all about me' mindset and start thinking about the employer. How are you going to help your leaders fulfill their vision, meet targets, and solve problems? If you can add value, they will be convinced that you are the best hire. Once you can demonstrate how you can help them achieve their goals through your experience, age would become immaterial.

However, if they are still unmoved by your abilities and want to focus solely on what year you were born in, then they might not be the ideal employers for you. I doubt anyone would want to be a part of an organization that behaves in such a discriminatory fashion. There will be other companies who would appreciate you for what you can do.

Q16. But what if I'm really too senior for the roles available?

Occasionally there are situations where seniority in your field means a smaller market and fewer roles. For instance, if you are the chief human resources officer of a global company, then your career options might be limited if you are seeking a similar or bigger role. Such niche opportunities are few and far between and you may have to uproot to a different location which might not be want you really want. In such an event, you may have to reinvent yourself.

For our senior clients who have had enough of the rat race and the corporate jungle, they may choose to 'unbundle' their skills and experiences, offering them on an assignment basis for consulting projects. Many of them take on small scale projects for a good fee, working on their own terms, and can be quite selective about their clients. As mentioned earlier, we call this 'having a portfolio career' where you can choose to work on projects you enjoy.

Never assume that age is a barrier to your employment. There are probably many other reasons why you were not hired. You're only as old as you feel. If you feel old, you will project it unintentionally and the hiring manager will sense that.

Q17. What can you tell me about gigs?

Let's define the difference between Jobs and Gigs.

A job is a specific role you have within a company that you do every day. It's a permanent arrangement that can be in many forms—hourly, salaried, task or project based. And a job ends when you decide to move on, or when the company terminates your employment for whatever reason. A gig is a job with a limited shelf life. It's a term originally used in describing musicians who perform for a limited period at a venue. All gigs are jobs, but not all jobs are gigs. Today, all work is becoming more gig-like. It's rare to have one-job-for-life situations now. In fact, when we see someone who has been loyal to his company for more than 20 years, recruiters often question whether this person is adaptable. With the gig economy, people can work on a variety of projects at any one time. Sometimes even inside an organization, the work is gig-like. Which is why we have been preaching the need for Career Agility, hence the name of our company.

Let's start with why you should consider a side gig. As you may be aware, one source of income may be insufficient. If you lose your job, you lose your source of income. We have met many retrenched individuals who are very stressed about having lost their jobs and are in a hurry to find another one because of financial pressures.

So, besides full-time employment, individuals can generate income from various ways: buy and rent out properties (if you're wealthy enough), invest, trade, or run an e-commerce business. One of our clients who is a risk and compliance manager with a major healthcare company does foreign exchange trading on his own time and makes an average of $2,000 per month extra income from about 10 hours of trading a week. What good returns!

One big reason for starting a side gig is that it could be something you always wanted to do, but didn't. Some people enjoy baking, but are not able to do it professionally because their full-time jobs pay better. But you can start something that you have always wanted to do, on a small scale. Even as a hobby or a part-time business, it's an activity that would nourish your soul.

As your reputation grows, this side gig can scale up into something bigger. Or when you retire from your full-time job, you can easily transition into your side gig.

One client started a small studio offering baking and cooking classes, regularly inviting specialists to run workshops or demos. She left her full-time job once her side gig caught on and she could make a decent income from it.

We are frequently asked for ideas for side gigs. We cannot tell our clients what to do, but we can help them look for clues. Review Chapter 9 and read the section on interests and passions. Some of our clients' side-gigs include giving piano lessons on weekends, stock trading, running a blogshop, creating content on YouTube, selling products online, and offering executive coaching. Some individuals have academic gigs, teaching evening and weekend classes.

These side gigs can sometimes transform into something you can do after retirement. It keeps your mind sharp, and you can continue to earn an income way into your golden years.

Here are some steps to starting your side gig.

Step 1: Analyze: Look into your motives, identify your opportunity, and check if you have the skills needed.

Step 2: Research: Do you require training, licensing, or certification? How much investment is required? Like starting a small business, you will need to evaluate the market and determine the costs, returns, and risks.

Step 3: Plan: How much time will you need to run your side gig? If you have a full-time job, you may only have the weekends and evenings available for it.

Ensure that there is no conflict of interest when running your side gig. This could be in terms of your time and any intellectual property you might create in the process. We do not encourage starting a business that competes with your own employer.

Q18. What is the best job search activity that yields the biggest result?

That's simple. It's all about networking actively. Get out into the market and start speaking to people. These could include headhunters, recruiters, your ex-bosses, former colleagues and even your competitors. Let them know you are seeking other opportunities. Networking also allows the hiring manager to get to know you, even before there is an official job opening. If the hiring manager knows you or has worked with you before, you might end up being the preferred candidate.

Be alert for when your network tells you about a problem or an issue. Listen, empathize, and offer help. Ideally, you would have already built a reputation for excellence in your domain and are a subject matter expert in your chosen area. Networking helps you access the hidden job market and get in ahead of the curve before the company even places a job advertisement.

Q19. Why are hiring managers ignoring my resume?

There could be many reasons why your target audience is not responding to your job applications. Here are a few possible reasons.

You are spamming your recipients. Recruiters receive countless number of unsolicited emails and CVs daily. Faced with the deluge of CVs, they have devised their own algorithm as to whether a CV gets responded to, filed, or trashed. Unsolicited CVs are often deleted on the spot, especially those without context. Refrain from this behaviour as it is a major source of annoyance for hiring managers and it will earn you a bad reputation with them.
You are applying for roles that you are either unqualified or overqualified for. Often this happens when insufficient homework is done on the role, or perhaps you might not be reading the job description correctly. Sometimes, an ambiguous job title like 'HR

Advisor' can mean an entry level position or a senior leadership position. Read the fine print and other details to understand fully what the company is looking for.

You are sending the application to the wrong person. Sometimes, you might send your CV to the person you think is making the important decisions, but unfortunately isn't. Often HR administrators are the first in line to assess and filter applicants who seem like a fit and exclude others who aren't. These gatekeepers sometimes do not fully understand the strategic requirements of the hiring manager and if your complicated profile does not seem to fit their image of the ideal candidate, your CV goes straight to the trash folder.

Find out who the decision makers are and send your CV directly to them. This information is often readily available on LinkedIn, so do your homework well!

Q20. Why do interviewers sometimes ask silly questions?

'How do you know if a tree is stable?' (Google)
'How many lamp-posts are there from the airport to our office?' (BP)
'What would you do if you became the Minister for Tourism?' (Shell)

These are actual interview questions used by hiring managers.

The main purpose is often to judge how you respond to an unexpected situation and how you react when put in a spot. However, many times, these frivolous questions are used to examine your thought processes and how you think.

For instance, if you responded to the last question with something frivolous like 'I would increase tourist numbers by putting up big banners welcoming visitors at our airport!', it does not highlight your intellect in the most flattering manner.

(Why would you put banners *inside the airport?* Haven't the visitors *already arrived?)* Remember that there is never a right or wrong answer to these types of questions. The interviewer just wants to observe your thought processes.

Q21. If there are three interviewers, who do I make the most eye contact with?

Respond to the interviewer asking the questions, but do not forget to also make eye contact with the others. Do not ignore anyone for you can never know if the quiet and unassuming lady sitting in the corner is the secretary or the global head of HR. If there are more than three interviewers, make a conscious effort to look in the direction of all of them as you are talking, trying hard not to make anyone feel left out.

Q22. What should I never do in an interview?

You should never speak badly of your ex-boss or former company, no matter how miserably they might have treated you in the past. This is a very serious faux pas which basically tells your potential boss that they may receive the same treatment from you when you leave their employment.

Keep it professional. Avoid talking about religious viewpoints, politics, or controversial issues. These divisive topics should not factor into your ability to do the job, and if you are asked your opinions during the interview, politely decline to answer.

The biggest mistake is going in unprepared. You do not want to try winging the interview. If you really want the job badly, do your homework on the company and their products. We have seen candidates talk at length about a product range that was discontinued a year ago. It was like watching a trainwreck in slow motion. To leave a positive impression to your interviewers, appear knowledgeable to demonstrate interest in the role and the company.

Q23. What question do I ask the interviewer?

In lawyer-themed TV shows, the older, more experienced lawyer will always tell the junior one, 'When in front of the judge/jury, never ask the witness a question you don't already know the answer to'.

Similarly, the 'So, do you have any questions?' part of the interview can be a good opportunity to reinforce additional points about your profile and abilities.

For instance, you can ask, *'What are the most important attributes needed to succeed in this role?'*

The hiring manager would then rattle off a list of competencies and after he is done, you can respond with 'Yes, attributes A, B, and C are indeed critical for this role. That's why I'm quite comfortable with it as I have <insert your achievements highlighting attribute A, B, and C here>'.

You get the picture.

Q24. Do you have any tips about interviewing via videoconferencing?

Today, interviews conducted via videoconferencing are common. We have grown comfortable talking into the PC, hence I would like to remind you of the following tips to help you through this.

Technical considerations

Turn your camera on and make sure you are at eye level and centred. Ensure adequate lighting on your face and do a soundcheck before the interview itself. Dress appropriately and not just the top half if you are at home.

Speak slowly.

Often, the person at the other end of the line may not be of the same nationality or culture as you, hence he may not comprehend you at your usual talking speed. Moreover, the internet connection may not be stable and the transmission may not be perfect. Slow down and enunciate each word carefully to avoid misunderstandings.

Make sure there are no background noises.

Ensure you are in a quiet place with a strong Wi-Fi signal. You do not want to be distracted during the session or suffer an intermittent connection that could throw you off your game.

Be prepared.

Sometimes, you are scheduled to speak with someone in a different time-zone. It could even be at 6.00 a.m. your local time. *Do wake up at least a half hour before to fully come to your senses.*

Q25. There is a job I really want. Can I suggest a pay cut to make myself more attractive?

No. Do not ever do that! When hiring managers hear candidates say, 'I'm willing to take a pay cut,' warning bells go off. The idea that you're willing to give a discount on yourself does not increase the employer's trust and confidence. Moreover, it makes you sound desperate.

There are other ways of mitigating this situation. For instance, if you find that you are indeed 'overpriced' for a role you really want, you could suggest a lower base salary and pinning the rest of your remuneration upon the completion of the project or when assigned targets are achieved.

This requires a fair bit of strategy development and salary negotiation, so you might want to speak to your career coach about this.

Q26. What should I do before accepting the offer?

So, they have finally made you an offer and all that is needed to seal the deal is your signature on the offer letter. But before you sign on the dotted line, pause, take a step back, and ask yourself these questions.

Will this opportunity improve my life?

Will this new job make me happier or more satisfied with my career? Is it going to positively affect my self-confidence, health, and family life? If the new role is going to bring about more stress and/or disharmony to your family relationships, you need to think really hard about accepting it.

Have you checked with your spouse?

A change in job is a major decision and will affect the entire family. Have you spoken to your spouse/partner about it? Is he/she supportive of the move? The new role may require longer hours and increased travel—will this impact your family?

Does this move fit into your Career Strategy?

Is it in line with your future goals two jobs down the road and does it leverage your strengths, interests, and skills? Is this industry you are getting into a growth or a sunset one? Is there better career progression at this new company compared to your current one? How will this role improve and enhance your ongoing career story?

Have you done your due diligence on the company and your future boss?

Are you familiar with the company's future strategy or product line-up? Are they financially stable? Have they been reorganizing their business units/teams repeatedly over the last few years (a very big red flag)? Is your future boss easy to work with? You need to have a good understanding of your new environment to minimize any sudden shocks after joining the new team.

Will there be a good cultural fit?

Different companies have different cultures and, sometimes, it is challenging to adapt to the new one if the changes are too drastic. We know of a senior candidate who spent two decades in progressive MNCs who suddenly decided to join a competitor. The consensus-seeking culture was not suited to him and he quit after three months.

Have you met your team members yet?

A lot of your success depends on your colleagues and team members. Having difficult teammates can sink your hopes for a successful transition very quickly. We have heard horror stories of candidates who turn up on the first day of work only to find a team of resentful staff who were unhappy that the job went to an 'outsider' and wanted to prove that the appointment was a bad mistake. Meeting the team and understanding their strengths and weaknesses enable you to make a better decision as to whether you want to join the new company.

Am I clear on my KPIs, goals, scope, geography, and degree of travel?

Even though things may change after you sign up, it is important that you have clarity on how you will be assessed, the extent of regional coverage, and the teams you will work with. This will reduce any confusion when you start the job.

Am I comfortable with the salary and/or performance bonus scheme?

Have the terms of compensation been made clear to you, or are there parts of the contract you are still unsure of?

Are you certain of the details and breakdown of employee benefits? Are you comfortable with the KPIs upon which your annual performance bonus will be based? These important details need to be sorted out with HR before you sign the offer letter.

Q27. How do I know the value system of the company I'm joining?

You have identified your values. The question now is 'How does knowing my values help me find out if there is a good fit with my potential employer?'

Here are some practical tips on how to find out your potential employer's values.

Ask the people who work there what it is like.

You may meet these individuals as a part of your networking or during a peer interview. You may get cautious if politically correct statements like 'The work is great but the environment can be very challenging' are thrown around. Listen carefully and clarify what they mean. Sometimes you have to listen for what is not said. The word 'challenge' could be a euphemism for 'really tough and unpleasant work'.

Ask ex-employees what their experience was like.

They are more likely to share openly. Recently exited employees are a good source of information, both positive and negative. Ask insightful questions and probe deeply to find relevant information.

Ask open-ended questions.

For example, if you value teamwork, do not ask 'Is teamwork important in your company?' You will get an instant 'Of course, it is!' Instead, you should ask something like this 'Can you share what you do to help your team members bond? Like, are there any activities to help keep the camaraderie strong?'

Gathering all the feedback will give you an understanding of the company's values, your potential reporting manager's values, and ultimately the culture of the workplace. If you do decide to join the company, you now know what to look out for and how to navigate the dynamics of the workplace.

Q28. What factors can I use to negotiate for a better salary?

Before you even begin salary negotiations, you need to recognize the contributing factors that determine your offer package. This will empower you to negotiate on each factor to build a compelling case as to why you should command a premium over the next candidate.

These factors are summarized below:

Demand for your skill/network/knowledge

Your value to the company is usually the sum total of the skill, network, knowledge, and expertise that you can bring to them. If the skills that you have are rare and your market knowledge is deeper than the other candidates, your bargaining power increases.

Your track record

Having a particularly valuable skill won't matter if you do not have a recent track record of success in that area. You may have been a top surgeon, but if your last five patients died on your operating table, you might have a tough time convincing people you are really good at what you do. Highlight your stellar track record and you will have an easier time negotiating your salary.

Your years of relevant experience

Malcolm Gladwell, in his book *Outliers*, suggested that it takes around 10,000 hours to fully master a skill. Hence, the more experience you have at the job or in the industry, the more confidence the employer has in your ability to do it well. Be ready to list your extensive experience at the interview.

Your qualifications

For certain technical roles or specialized industries, having specific certifications can add a premium to your candidature. Sometimes, having a 'branded' degree from Harvard, Oxford, or MIT further enhances your positioning for the job.

The amount of work involved

Is the role a local, regional, or a global one? Salary bands increase with similar increases in scope and if the job is going to keep you up all night with conference calls to some distant country across the globe, there must be a premium.

Besides geographic scope, other considerations include whether this role is that of an individual contributor or a manager.

Often, salary is commensurate with the revenue size of the business too—a person handling a $50 million business will not command as high a package as someone in charge of a $500 million one.

Your employer's budget

No matter how qualified you may be for a role, the final package is often dictated by the company's budget. A corporate client of ours has a policy of paying top dollar for top performers, believing that you have to pay for quality and can be flexible and creative in terms of remuneration for the right candidates. We have also seen companies who stick rigidly to the budget set up by HR and no amount of negotiation can alter what has already been cast in stone.

Know what your bargaining chips are before you even sit down at the table, and you will stand a better chance of getting a good deal.

Q29. Should I accept a counteroffer after I have tendered my resignation?

So, you've signed the letter of offer with your dream company, and you've informed your bosses about it. Naturally, they are unhappy and will try their best to retain you. In a desperate attempt to make you change your decision, they may offer a handsome salary increase, a fancier job title, or even the corner office with a view.

We always get asked, 'Should I accept the counteroffer?'

Here are some uncomfortable truths you need to consider before you accept it.

Does your company really treasure your services or are they buying time before they get a replacement for you?

Often, the counteroffer serves as a delay tactic for companies to stall until your replacement can be found. Once you have signaled your intention to leave, you are a known flight-risk and a liability to their operations, and the process of getting your replacement will commence. Because it takes roughly six months to get a new person on board, they would still need you for now, hence the counteroffer. We have seen far too many candidates fall prey to this tactic, only to be fired six months down the road when their replacement arrives.

Why does the company give you a raise only when you threaten to resign?

Are they being sincere? Most counteroffers can be generous. This may be tempting, but ask yourself this: why weren't you worth that much to them yesterday? Will you have to repeat the threat every time there is a salary review meeting for the rest of your career? What type of company do you work for if they only give you what you are worth when you threaten to resign?

If you accept the counteroffer, how will you be perceived in the organization?

Your bosses will still think of you as a flight-risk and your colleagues may paint you as an attention seeker. Your reputation and personal pride will take a blow because, truth be told, you were bought. Accepting a counteroffer could suggest that you were not really looking for a job in the first place but that you were simply itching for a raise. Once the word gets out, the relationship that you now enjoy with your co-workers will never be the same again.

Are you aware of the real risk of accepting a counteroffer?

Anecdotal evidence suggests that those who accept a counteroffer usually end up leaving the company within six months, either of their own volition or are fired.

When it comes to that stage, you have effectively burned your bridges with both your employer (you threatened to leave them!) as well as the company which you turned down (you reneged on their letter of offer!).

So, the harsh reality is that accepting a counteroffer from your employers carries a lot of risk.

Our frank advice is to make up your mind 100% before signing the letter of offer. Commit yourself to the move, then make an unshakeable decision to notify your bosses that you are leaving.

Q30. I am thinking of joining a start-up. What should I look out for?

Joining a start-up can be an exciting experience, but before you quit your job and sign up with that promising company that just called, you need to consider these points before you make that life-changing move.

Are you ready for it?

Start-ups are renowned for their frenetic pace of work and often entails long and arduous hours at the office and also at home.

'I've never worked so hard before in my life, not even in my fresh-graduate days! It was a total shock!' said Michael, a 46-year-old banker turned product manager. 'I was almost burnt out by the second month!'

'I also had to adjust to working with teammates who were half my age. I had to match their pace, lingo, and energy levels which was both invigorating and exciting. It offered me an insight into this new work dynamic,' he added.

The biggest thing you have to be ready for is that joining a start-up is inherently risky. There are never any guarantees that the company will survive the foreseeable future as even the disruptors themselves get unceremoniously disrupted by a more aggressive start-up.

Is the business model viable?

This is one of the biggest questions you need to ask yourself. Does it pass the 'Yeah, I'd pay for that with my own money' test? Is this service or product something you would buy and be so excited about that you would recommend it to all your family and friends? Or is it a novelty that would fade into oblivion once people get bored with it?

You also need to figure out if the business is sustainable. Will it still be around in one year's time? Does it have enough cash to last until the next round of financing?

You can probably get their funding details off the internet, and a quick eyeball of staff-strength and costs will give you an idea of their 'burn rate'. So, even with a $1 million seed fund, a start-up with a 3,000 square foot office and a team of 40 programmers will run out of cash in under 6 months.

Also, is the start-up competing with a known giant?

For example, at Career Agility International, we often get invited to work with ambitious start-ups that want to build a better resume repository or professional networking platform like LinkedIn. Unless they have a uniquely different approach, competing directly with LinkedIn does not make commercial sense for us. The moment you feel that the business model does not make sense, walk away.

What type of package are they offering you?

If you are a senior executive, the start-up probably can't afford you. As such, in exchange for a reduced salary, they will offer you stock options or equity to entice you to join them. At this point in time, stories of early-stage pioneers like Jobs, Bezos, or Zuckerberg will come flooding into your mind as you eagerly sign on the dotted line.

However, for every Apple Inc, there are hundreds of Oric Computers and Commodore Inc that fell by the wayside. Your stocks wouldn't be worth anything in these situations.

Also, some companies will offer you stock options which allow you to buy the publicly traded shares at steep discounts when the company gets its IPO (Initial Public Offering) and is listed. Do note that these options are worthless if there isn't an IPO and cannot be exercised in a 'trade-sale' where the company is bought by a bigger corporation. As there's no listing, there's no value attached.

Instead, try asking for direct equity, as in a percentage share of the business so that whenever the investors exit in whatever format, you will get still a piece of the action. Granted, many entrepreneurs are unwilling to split their equity with you, so you will need to learn how to negotiate your way in. Though difficult, the reward could be tremendous.

Will you fit in well?

It is not a cliché to say that many start-ups are founded and run by younger people. This has implications with regards to the way they work, their values, and even the way they communicate. Will you be a good fit with their culture, especially if you come from a very structured, well-organized multinational company.

'I had such a difficult time acclimatizing to their way of working—there were no systems, no processes, and the CEO made decisions on the fly without approvals or debate. I felt I was out of my element, said Harry, 43, who spent his career at an oil major before moving to a start-up.

Also, be prepared to report to a supervisor who could be much younger than you and collaborate with colleagues who have lived fewer years than you have been working. Are you ready to put your ego aside and take instructions from them?

Do you like the CEO?

As you will probably be working very closely with the founders and especially the CEO, it is imperative that you have a good chemistry or a working relationship with them. Are you comfortable with their workstyle, methods of communication, or management ability? Do your values align?

We once had a client who left after a short three-month stint at a start-up because the CEO was a micromanager and was unbearably difficult to work with.

This is exactly why you need to meet with the people you will be working with and get comfortable with them before you sign the offer letter.

Moving to a start-up is an exciting opportunity that should not be dismissed quickly. Neither should it be hastily rushed into. The risks are high, but so is the reward, and the journey would be a memorable one. There will be new and exciting skills to be learnt and friends to be made.

Many of the new skills you pick up can be transferred to your next role and the new connections you've made can be of value to your future company, hence it could be a great career opportunity.

Make the move with both eyes open. Ask the right questions, do your homework, and be prepared for the adventure of a lifetime!

Q31. Should I get my MBA?

With the increasing number of graduates today, many have considered getting an MBA to differentiate themselves from the crowd and also to update or upgrade their skills. If you are toying with the idea of embarking on an MBA journey, here is some advice you might want to consider.

Take your MBA earlier in your career.

The opportunity costs are lower and you will probably enjoy better returns as you have a longer career ahead of you. However, there are those who argue that earning your MBA without having real-life work experience under your belt works against you. So, it has been said that the ideal age to obtain an MBA should be between 32–38 years old.

Don't waste your time getting an MBA from an 'unknown' or 'unbranded' university.

A Harvard or a Stanford MBA trumps an MBA from an online university anytime.

If your employer has to ask, *'The what university?'*, the value to your credentials may not justify the amount of money and time you have invested. So, make sure you are investing in a good university—one that's going to add to your brand.

Leverage your MBA as much as you can.

Network and build relationships with your course-mates. You never know when they may be your future clients/bosses/colleagues.

Network with your alumni—you have just been inducted into a very exclusive fraternity, so actively reach out to past graduates. Attend your alumni events regularly and make it a point to meet new people. Learn what they do and find out how you can help them. Be genuine in your outreach.

Can I afford the program?

MBAs can be an expensive venture. The fees range from US $50,000 to as much as a US $150,000 for a branded program. This does not include the associated costs of living overseas and does not factor in the opportunity cost of not working for the next 12–24 months. In all, expect to invest at least US $100,000 to US $250,000 for your MBA.

So, the next question that many people ask is, 'Can I make that back?'.

The truth is that if you have done your homework, you probably will. But the right question to ask should be 'How long will I actually take to break even on the investment?'.

Do your numbers carefully.

Do you have enough money to last you beyond the duration of study? You might want to factor in a 3–6 months buffer after you have graduated just in case you don't get a job immediately upon graduation. You might also want to budget for the holidays and side trips you will take during the term-breaks.

MBAs are expensive affairs—make sure you budget well and have healthy savings on standby.

Get buy-in from your spouse before you commence.

Studying for your MBA is a full-time commitment, even if you are doing it part-time. The long hours needed for group projects and assignments can take a toll on your relationships if not properly managed. Finances can also be strained when, suddenly, a dual-income couple becomes a single-income one. Obtaining your MBA should be a joint decision simply because it is a major life event that affects both partners.

In general, many employers regard an MBA as an important part of a Senior Executive's development, and it often improves your employability. However, we have seen employers who value relevant work experience more than on-paper qualifications. So, consider all these facts before you sign up for that MBA programme.

Q32. When can I retire?

Not many people plan what will happen when they retire. Besides financial considerations, most do not think about what they want to do with their time. They may jokingly say, 'I want to travel the world!' or, 'I'll do nothing!' You can't travel all the time forever and you cannot be doing nothing forever.

Review Chapter 9 on self-assessment. List your interests. Start incubating ideas so that the transition into actual retirement is smoother.

For example, we have clients who say they want to teach once they retire from their full-time jobs. Unfortunately, once they are ready to teach, there are no roles waiting for them. They have not carved a niche, actively engaged with the academic institutions or professional associations, and no one knows who they are.

It takes time to incubate such a strategy. They have to already be an active member of the associations or a regular guest speaker at academic institutions. As a known entity with highly visible proof of domain expertise, teaching opportunities become viable.

Of course, not all retirement gigs require incubation. Some just want to start a hobby or to volunteer their time. Do take the time to plan for it anyway, as it would make the transition smoother.

Part H

Conclusion

14

Conclusion

Many of us are defined by our careers, and our career is one of the greatest assets that we own. In these chapters, we have learnt how to embrace our career, nurture our career, and bring our career to new levels by focusing on the twin goals of career planning: career longevity and career satisfaction. We also learned that both can only be achieved by developing our Career Strategy and having the Career Agility to act on it.

We need to realize that our career is a 40-year journey that we undertake from our 20s to our late 60s. So, it needs to be managed and curated with the appropriate strategies at every stage along the way. However, we also need to be reminded that our careers are only a subset of who we truly are. We are more than just our jobs, our companies, or the work we do. So, we need to focus on what is truly important to us—our relationships, our health, and our purpose in life.

Thank you for reading this book as it has been a blessing to be able to share our ideas with you.

We wish you a great career ahead!

Adrian and Yen

Part I

Appendices

Appendix A: What Career Animal are you?

Over the past 20 years, we have spoken to thousands of executives around the world about their careers and how they've been managing their Career Strategy. Common themes and behaviours came up and we've identified 4 broad categories. For simplicity (and fun), we have decided to name them after different animals.

There are neither good groups nor bad groups, as each has the potential to shine even brighter, but some groups are at bigger risk of disruption in this insane post-Covid-19 market.

Each group needs special strategies to cope with the challenges ahead, and knowing which Career Animal you are allows you to deploy the correct career strategies specific to your situation. As you read each of these descriptions, see if you can identify people within your professional circle who display each of these characteristics.

The Lion

A Career Lion is an individual who stands proud, is agile, and adaptable to the environment around him. He knows where to hunt for new opportunities, and when his domain runs out of prey, he will move on to richer hunting grounds to stay ahead of his competition.

Career Lions rank high on the Career Strategy spectrum for their ability to plan ahead, and aligning their short-term decisions to their long-term career plans. They also rank highly on the agility spectrum for their ability to navigate change, leverage opportunities, mitigate threats, and adapt to any situational changes. They probably have a high-interest level in their chosen vocations and are well connected, which would keep them very updated in their market.

An example of a Career Lion is Steve Jobs who co-founded Apple in 1976, and mass-produced full GUI Macintosh computers. When he was forced out of Apple in 1985, he founded NeXT and Pixar, which went on to become a major animation studios. He became the CEO of Apple in 1997 and was largely credited for helping revive and rescue it from the brink of bankruptcy, creating innovative personal devices in the following decade. He was able to spot trends, seize opportunities, stay resilient, and remain agile in his career for over four decades.

The Canary

A Career Canary is someone who is agile but have been in their cage (job or company) for many years, they have forgotten how to fly. Safe in the confines of their gilded cage, even when great opportunities present themselves at the door, they will turn their back on it, choosing the comfort and safety of what is known.

Career Canaries rank high on the agility spectrum, which indicates that they have the adaptability and skills to do well in their careers, but due to a variety of reasons, do not rank highly on the strategy spectrum. Some of the most common reasons for this are fear of the unknown, too comfortable to want to make a change or try new things, and lack of market awareness.

An example of a Career Canary would be **Jeff Immelt**, the former CEO of General Electric. Despite a long career in GE, he couldn't really fully adapt to the world outside when he was retired from the company in 2017.

The T-Rex

A Career T-Rex has lots of grand plans and ambitions but is unable to fulfill them because he does not have the agility, skill, or knowledge to execute them. Overly confident on the outside but feeling frustrated and insecure on the inside, he realizes that there are opportunities that are just beyond the reach of his short, tiny hands. He will see opportunities present themselves, then slide away as he tries again and again to land them.

Career T-Rexes may be passed over for promotions and career advancement opportunities, and not know why. While they feel they are suited for the role, they lack the agility to position themselves for the opportunity.

Nicola Tesla, the famous inventor of the alternating current, was such a T-Rex. Even though he had lot of grand plans for his groundbreaking creations, only a few made it to market. He never reached the level of commercial success that his rival Thomas Edison did because he did not have the Career Agility to achieve it.

The Panda

A Career Panda is someone who has been too comfortable with his career over the years and has become fat, immobile, and endangered. Unable to adapt to changes in temperature, they prefer not to venture out into areas that might cause them discomfort.

Their narrow diet of bamboo shoots restricts their adaptability to other environments and greener pastures. Career Pandas can be identified in many large organizations by their lack of enthusiasm, outdated skillsets, and difficulty adjusting to new technologies or changes. Career Pandas are often at risk of being retrenched. Career Pandas score low on both the strategy and the agility spectrums. They lack the skills and motivation to further or progress their careers. Some career pandas can thrive because their environment is stable, and as long as the organization structure doesn't change, they can happily continue with the status quo for decades. However, the corporate environment is a dynamic one, and some changes and shake-ups can be drastic. Organizations can be acquired, restructured, split, and some even implode. The resulting fallout may see many Career Pandas displaced, and worse remain unemployable.

One such Panda is **Antonio Perez**, the CEO of Kodak, who refused to come out of his comfort zone (the camera film industry) and switch to digital camera technology, which he described as a 'crappy business'. The company filed for Chapter 11 in 2012 under him.

So, what now?

To figure out what Career Animal you are, we have an offer for you at the end of this book. You can take the CAROL (Career Agility and Resilience Online) quiz and you will receive a detailed report which includes some advice on how to navigate your career.

The diagnosis is not a life sentence. It is a snapshot of a moment in your career journey and your current frame of mind. Do not fret if the results are not ideal. There is no right and wrong, and there is no point in trying the Career Agility index multiple times to achieve a better result. That is not its goal.

The ultimate objective is to give you some level of awareness that your career journey needs a driver who is paying attention.

That driver is you. As the pilot and captain, you are responsible for making your own career decisions. As with any journey, you sometimes need to pause to ask for directions, stop and check if your pace is good, and also look out for obstacles or blind spots. For that, do seek advice from mentors and coaches.

Your CAROL results can be a good starting point for you to have conversations with your mentors, supervisors, leaders, and peers. Based on these conversations, you can now create a long-term Career Strategy and some short-term career goals to drive your career in the direction you want. You may want to re-take the quiz again in a year or two, just as another career health check.

Appendix B: My Career Story—
Adrian Choo, the Author

As I turn 50 this year, I look back at a series of rather serendipitous twists that have brought me to where I am today, running the World's first career-strategy consultancy Career Agility International.

I would categorize my career story into three phases: my school years, my early career, and my final pivot.

My School Years

As a young child, I had always been very fascinated by other people's careers. My dad was a humble administrative clerk in Standard Chartered Bank, a place where he worked for over 3 decades before retiring at 55.

My Mom was a 'housewife' (Yes, that's what they were called back in the 70s.) My older brother and I didn't have much, but we were living comfortably.

I was always curious about what *my friends'* parents' occupations were and was always amazed by how much *wealthier* they were than my family. A classmate's dad was a Singapore Airline pilot and he never failed to show off his annual vacation photos to Disneyland and Europe, even though the tickets were free!

I started exploring careers and by 13, I decided that I was going to be a doctor as I did well in Biology and had this amazing knack for remembering Latin terms. I was convinced that medical studies were the way forward for me.

However, as fate would have it, my brother, who is 5 years older than me, got into medical school and, one day, he sneaked me into the anatomy lab where first-year medical students dissected their freshly procured *cadavers*.

Yes . . . *dead human bodies*!

With youthful enthusiasm, I stepped into the dimly lit room and caught sight of rows of frightfully tanned, leathery, and shriveled bodies laid bare on cold steel gurneys. I was then greeted by the nauseating stench of formaldehyde (preserving fluid) and old, wet socks.

I turned around and ran out of the room, expelling my breakfast all over the corridor. I remember my brother laughing out loud behind me saying, 'If you can't handle this, a career in medicine is out of the question for you!'

He was correct, so I had to redefine my career aspirations. Then, I watched this movie starring Michael Douglas—*Wall Street*—and got fascinated with the world of business and high finance, especially with the main protagonist Gordon Gekko's speech about how *'Greed is good'*. I then decided to go into business.

So I immersed myself in books like *Odyssey, from Pepsi to Apple*, *How to Master the Art of Selling*, and even Trump's *Art of the Deal* (wouldn't recommend the last one, though).

When I turned 19 and was serving my national service in the Army, I decided to gain some hands-on experience in setting up a business. At that time, my brother's medical school classmates lamented the lack of *real human skeletons* that they needed to study anatomy, and plastic replicas weren't just detailed enough.

Responding to the market-gap, I started a business that sourced and imported medical-grade real human skeletons to sell to the local medical school freshmen. These bones were clean, odourless, and most importantly, legally/ethically sourced from certified medical institutions across Europe. Initially, I had issues identifying storage facilities to keep them, and ultimately, had to store them in my room. Once, I literally had about *a dozen skeletons in my closet.*

I ran this business even as I was studying at university and supported my own expenses throughout my 4 years at varsity, which was pretty cool as my classmates were wondering how I could afford driving my own car to school and own a nice mobile phone. This was the early 90s, cell phones weren't common then!

I had my first taste of business and thoroughly enjoyed it.

Interestingly, if it wasn't for this turn of events that led me to the exciting world of entrepreneurship, I would not have become what I am today.

Career Lessons I've Learned

1. You need to roll with the punches. Don't cast your career dreams in concrete. You need to be flexible and agile to adapt to changing situations.

2. Understand what 'fires you up'. What gets you excited? What brings you joy? Follow that angle and love what you do!

3. Keep learning. I didn't have any mentors until I was 30 and starting up without one was difficult. Find mentors and keep them close.

My Early Career

In life, there are 'sliding door' moments (like in the Gwyneth Paltrow movie *Sliding Doors*) where pivotal decisions make you who and what you become eventually.

My second moment came when I hit my first career crossroads at 30 years of age. Fresh out of a short but unsatisfying stint as a business development manager in GE Plastics, I felt very frustrated at my lack of career direction.

Flashing back 7 years prior, I was handpicked out of my faculty cohort to join Shell and had spent the early part of my career in that illustrious company. However, in 2000, the call of entrepreneurship became too loud to ignore, and I started my own Dotcom business—3 months before the technology bubble burst. We were funded by angel investors and ran the business for 3 years before I decided that the model was not scalable enough and handed it off to my partners to manage.

I, then, joined GE Plastics' industrial design division as their business development manager. The company developed and engineered cutting-edge designs for mobile phone and technology companies. Clients include HP, Dell, and other technology giants.

However, my role was only in hunting and bringing in new accounts. Because I was not an industrial designer, I could not deliver the services I sold. Being at the 'sales end' of the value-chain made me very insecure. Career-wise, I felt that being able to only catch (procure new clients) but not cook (deliver the engineering designs) put me at a huge disadvantage.

In my view, my role as a salesperson can always be replaced and because I was not able to deliver the solutions I sold, I would always have to depend on a company to create these solutions. I was effectively at the mercy of a corporation and had become 'company-dependent'.

To me, this imbalance of power made me career insecure and I sought a better career solution, one where I held all the cards. My ideal job had to:

1. be a profession where I could 'cook' whatever I 'caught'.
2. play to my strengths, passions, and temperament.
3. be in a growth market with huge upside.
4. value experience over youthful energy.
5. be something I would enjoy doing.

I literally spent a day by the beach on my 31st birthday to figure out my Career Strategy and I finally decided to enter the headhunting industry.

I discovered that being a headhunter, or more accurately, a retained executive search consultant was the answer to my career insecurity question. I could hunt for new business and execute the search myself, and best of all, I would be 'company-independent'. If ever I wanted to quit a firm, I would just leave and bring all my clients along with me—I could even start my own company if I wanted to.

My first step was to gain entry into a new industry and I networked actively toward that end. Within 3 months, I had two offers and took my time to evaluate my options. Eventually, I accepted an offer which involved a significant pay cut, but I believed that it was a good move. I was confident that with the commissions, I would be making even more money within eighteen months, but I did so in only eight.

In hindsight, there were some career lessons that I learned during this episode.

Career Lessons I've Learned

1. **Act quickly.** If you have to make a drastic career switch into a totally new area, do it when you are young, cheap, and more risk-tolerant, with fewer bills to pay. If you want to do it when you're older, make sure you have a career strategist to work out the details with you.

2. **Seek clarity.** Always seek to understand what exactly is bugging you. You need to have absolute clarity as to which aspect of your career you want to change, then go change it.

3. **Trust your strategy and move forward.** Once you have a Career Strategy mapped out, be bold and do whatever it takes, even if there's a salary cut. Be courageous and take educated risks.

My 12 years in headhunting were the most lucrative in my career and I never looked back. However, in 2012, I foresaw a storm brewing in the recruitment industry that could spell the end of the business as we knew it. Once again, I knew I had to take corrective action to avoid it.

The Final Pivot

The year was 2012 and I was having one of my best-performing streaks in my career. I was at the top of my game in the world of retained executive search, generating a lot of revenue, and enjoying every minute of it until I took a long and hard look at my industry, and the wise words of Jack Ma came flooding into my mind:

'*The best time to fix the roof is when it is not raining.*'

In a panic, I forced myself to highlight the three things that could or have already begun to disrupt my industry, and I identified three ominous signs.

1. LinkedIn was going to take away a significant portion of the recruitment industry,
2. Our fees and rates have been steadily declining since the Global Financial Crisis of 2008 as competition for a shrinking market heated up.
3. A trend of in-sourcing of talent acquisition was gaining momentum with major clients. They were building in-house recruitment teams to bypass external headhunters.

These three factors, though minor back in 2012, would only escalate in the next 8 years and if I had remained in the same space, I would become a dinosaur facing certain extinction. Headhunting was undoubtedly on the decline.

I then forced myself to review my own *Career Strategy* to explore what my next steps should be.

Once again, I prioritized my career goals as follows:

#1 Career longevity, means being in an industry that was growing and having the skills that would see continued demand for my service.

#2 Career scalability, means that in the long run, I would not be 'selling hours of my own time' (which had its limits), but rather a solution that could be replicated and scaled upwards.

#3 Career enjoyment, means that I will be doing what I love doing most, in my case, meeting people and helping them solve their complex problems.

I scanned my industry and decided that I was best suited for career coaching, having conducted elements of it during my headhunting career. So, that was it.

To reposition myself and build my credibility, I authored and published my first book *Career Crossroads—A Headhunter's Guide to Career Strategy* in 2015. This book was the amalgamation of all the career advice that my C-suite clients and candidates taught me over my decade-long experience interviewing them. It took me close to 2 years to write and publish it, but the effects were phenomenal in establishing myself as *The Career Strategist*.

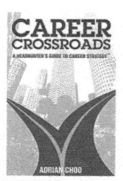

The popularity of the book got me noticed in the career coaching industry and I landed a role at an outplacement firm where I joined as their business development director.

From the first day I started work there, I had given myself a 3-year timeline to expose myself to as much of the industry as possible and then leave to start my coaching agency, and in Jan 2018, I walked out of the door, head held high, and started the world's first Career Agility coaching service.

Many people laughed at me when I told them what I had set out to achieve. One headhunting firm who tried to recruit me said, 'You'll come crawling back to us when your stupid idea fails.'

Today, I am blessed to have a wonderful team and a fantastic client base. The company enjoys excellent profitability and promising growth. Most importantly, I've achieved all three of my career goals (*longevity, scalability, and enjoyment*) and have found like-minded people to share it with.

So, if you are at a career crossroads and are unsure of what exactly you want, pause and start thinking of your career strategically and gain that clarity needed to achieve your career goals.

Do connect with me on LinkedIn: linkedin.com/in/adrianchoo.

Appendix C: My Career Story—Sze-Yen Chee, the Author

Growing up, I never really knew what I wanted to do, except to answer with the standard response, 'Lawyer, teacher, or doctor,' when asked.

With strong language, communication, and presentation skills, I gravitated towards journalism and public relations, but decided to pursue a Bachelor's in Business Administration for its wider offering of subjects and at a campus that was nearer home.

Yes, I loved the comforts of home.

I still had no idea which career path to pursue after four years of business school.

I recall having 11 jobs in a variety of industries before graduation—memorable stints in retail, hospitality, equities, telemarketing services, charities, and accounting.

With a high degree of clarity, I knew what I *didn't* want, and commenced the 'apply anywhere that did not make me shudder' strategy.

I went through several interviews and, during my last semester, received an offer from IBM which I accepted immediately, not because I was interested in technology, but because it meant I could get the job-search process done and begin planning my month-long trip overseas.

I realized very quickly that I could not thrive in an environment where I had to sell products or solutions I did not understand. With my sales and communication skills, I eventually transitioned into recruitment where I could see the impact on the people I helped. Interestingly, I never left the tech industry but refocused to an adjacent industry that made more sense to me.

Being in the recruitment industry, I witnessed many successful and unsuccessful career stories that piqued my interest in career coaching, something I would regularly do with candidates. Career coaching was a fairly new practice and was only discreetly offered to senior-level candidates who were retrenched. A business acquaintance asked me to facilitate a workshop on how to work with recruiters, speaking from a practicing recruiter's perspective. From that day, I knew I had found my niche. I decided to learn more and trained to get officially certified in that field.

My recruiting career was successful and lucrative. By then, I'd had 2 young children, and my husband had a job that required him to travel occasionally. With enough resources saved and family support, I transitioned into a portfolio career, facilitating career workshops and coaching.

As part of my Career Strategy, I have continued with my portfolio career till today, 17 years later and I am proud to say that I was able to be present for my 3 children in their challenging growing-up phases.

My Career Reflections:

• Work-life balance has always featured at the top of my values list. Family time has always been important to me. I have strived hard to ensure that my work fits into my personal life and not the other way around.

- I continuously invested in my professional development: courses, certifications, and a wide reading diet.
- Many of my portfolio gigs were found via networks. With my demonstrated track record in the work that I do, I have managed to maintain a sustainable practice.

I continue my mission in making a difference in people's lives and helping with their career concerns with Career Agility International.

Do connect with me on LinkedIn: linkedin.com/in/szeyen.

Appreciation

Authoring a book is a team effort and we wish to thank our Publisher, Penguin Random House, for this opportunity to share our ideas with the world.

We also wish to thank our team at Career Agility International Pte Ltd—Gabrielle, Valerie, and Rahm—for ideas that bring this book to life.

Special mention also goes to Dr Edwin Choo for his meticulous attention to detail in proofreading the manuscript.

Finally, our deepest thanks go out to our respective spouses—Ping and Alvin—whose support has made this endeavour possible.

Adrian and Yen

References

Bandura, A. 1977. *Social Learning Theory*. Englewood Cliffs, NJ: Prentice Hall.

Betz, N.E., Fitzgerald, L.F, and Hill, R.E. 1989. 'Trait-factor theories: Traditional cornerstone of career theory'. *Handbook of Career Theory*, edited by B. Michael, D.T. Hall, and B.S. Lawrence. New York: Cambridge University Press.

Bolles, R.N. 2019. *What Color Is Your Parachute? 2020: A Practical Manual for Job-Hunters and Career-Changers*. Ten Speed Press; Reprint Edition.

Brown, D. 1996. 'Introduction to theories of career development and choice' ed. by D. Brown and L. Brooks. *Career Choice and Development* 3rd ed. San Francisco, CA: Jossey-Bass.

Brown, D. 2002. *Career Choice and Development* 4th ed. San Francisco, CA: Jossey–Bass.

Brown, S.D., and Lent, R.T. 2005. *Career Development and Counseling: Putting Theory and Research to Work*. Hoboken, NJ: Wiley.

Capra, F. 1982. *The Turning Point: Science, Society, and the Rising Culture*. NY: Simon & Schuster.

Chen, C. 2003. 'Integrating perspectives in career development theory and practice'. *The Career Development Quarterly* 51: 203–216.

Choo, A. and Chee, S.Y. 2019. *7 Proven Secrets to Landing your Dream Job*. eBook. Career Agility International Pte Ltd.

Choo, A. and Chee, S.Y. 2019. *Accelerate Your Career*. eBook. Career Agility International Pte Ltd.

Choo, A. and Chee, S.Y. 2019. *The Exit Management Handbook—The Definitive Guide to Compassionate Retrenchment Practices.* Candid Creation Publishing, Singapore

Dawis, R.V., and Lofquist, L.H. 1984. *A Psychological Theory of Work Adjustment.* Minneapolis, MN: University of Minnesota Press.

Dobson, M.S. and Dobson, D.S. 2000. *Managing Up: Ways to Build a Career-Advancing Relationship with Your Boss.* AMACOM.

Ford, D., and Lerner, R. 1992. *Developmental Systems Theory: An Integrative Approach.* Newbury Park, CA: Sage.

Ford, M. 1992. *Motivating Humans: Goals, Emotions, and Personal Agency Beliefs.* Newbury Park, CA: Sage.

Ford, M., and Ford, D. 1987. *Humans as Self-Constructing Living Systems: Putting the Framework to Work.* Hillsdale, NJ: Lawrence Erlbaum.

Friedman, T.L. 2006. *The World is Flat: A Brief History of the Twenty–First Century Updated and Expanded.* New York: Farrar, Straus and Giroux.

Goldman, L. 1992. 'Qualitative assessment: An approach for counselors'. *Journal of Counseling and Development* 70: 616–621.

Gottfredson, L.S. 1981. 'Circumscription and compromise: A developmental theory of occupational aspirations'. *Journal of Counseling Psychology* 28: 545–579.

Gottfredson, L.S. 1996. 'Gottfredson's theory of circumscription and compromise'. *Career Choice and Development: Applying Contemporary Approaches to Practice* 3rd ed., edited by D. Brown and L. Brooks. San Francisco, CA: Jossey–Bass: 179–232.

Gottfredson, L.S. 2002. Gottfredson's theory of circumscription, compromise, and self–creation. *Career Choice and Development* 4th ed., edited by D. Brown and Associate. San Francisco, CA: Jossey–Bass: 85–148.

Granvold, D.K. 1996. 'Constructivist psychotherapy'. *Families in Society: The Journal of Contemporary Human Services* 77: 345–359.

Griffin, B., and Hesketh, B. 2003. 'Adaptable behaviours for successful work and career adjustment'. *Australian Journal of Psychology* 55: 65–73.

Gysbers, N.C., Heppner, M.J., and Johnston, J.A. 1998. *Career counseling: Process, Issues and Techniques.* Needham Heights, MA: Allyn and Bacon.

Hackett, G. 1993. 'Career counseling and psychotherapy: False dichotomies and recommended remedies'. *Journal of Career Assessment* 1: 105–117.

Hackett, G., and Betz, N.E. 1981. 'A self–efficacy approach to career development of women'. *Journal of Vocational Behaviour* 18: 326–339.

Herr, E.L. 1997. 'Perspectives on career guidance and counselling in the 21st century'. *Educational and Vocational Guidance* 60: 1–15.

Herr, E.L. 1997. 'Super's life–span, life–space approach and its outlook for refinement'. *The Career Development Quarterly* 45: 238–245.

Hesketh, B., and Rounds, J. 1995. 'International cross–cultural approaches to career development'. *Handbook of Vocational Psychology: Theory, Research, and Practice* 2nd ed., edited by W.B. Walsh and S.H. Osipow. Mahwah, NJ: Erlbaum: 367–390.

Holland, J.L. 1958. 'A personality inventory employing occupational titles'. *Journal of Applied Psychology* 42: 336–342.

Holland, J.L. 1959. 'A theory of vocational choice'. *Journal of Counseling Psychology* 6: 35–45.

Holland, J.L. 1973. *Making Vocational Choices*. Englewood Cliffs, NJ: Prentice Hall.

Holland, J.L. 1975. *Manual for the Vocational Preference Inventory*. Palo Alto, CA: Consulting Psychologists Press.

Holland, J.L. 1978. *The Occupations Finder*. Odessa, FL: Psychological Assessment Resources.

Holland, J.L. 1985. *Making Vocational Choices: A Theory of Vocational Personalities and Work Environments*. Englewood Cliffs, NJ: Prentice Hall.

Holland, J.L. 1994. *The Self-Directed Search* 4th ed. Odessa, FL: Psychological Assessment Resources.

Holland, J.L. 1996. 'Exploring careers with a typology: What we have learned and some new directions'. *American Psychologist* 51: 397–406.

Holland, J.L. 1996. *The Occupations Finder*. Odessa, FL: Psychological Assessment Resources.

Holland, J.L. 1997. *Making vocational choices: A theory of vocational personalities and work environments* 3rd ed. Odessa, FL: Psychological Assessment Resources.

Holland, J.L. 1997. *Making vocational choices: A theory of vocational personalities and work environments* 3rd ed. Odessa, FL: Psychological Assessment Resources.

Holland, J.L., and Gottfredson, G.D. 1994. *CASI: Career Attitudes and Strategies Inventory: An Inventory for Understanding Adult Careers.* Odessa, FL: Psychological Assessment Resources.

Holland, J.L., Daiger, D.C., and Power, P.G. 1980. *My Vocational Situation.* Palo Alto, CA: Consulting Psychologists Press.

Holland, J.L., Fritzsche, B.A., and Powell, A.B. 1994. *The Self-Directed Search Technical Manual.* Odessa, FL: Psychological Assessment Resources.

Killeen, J., White, M., and Watts, A.G. 1992. *The Economic Value of Careers Guidance.* London: Policy Studies Institute.

Krumboltz, J.D. 1993. 'Integrating career counseling and personal counseling'. *The Career Development Quarterly* 42: 143–148.

Lent, R.W. 2005. 'A social cognitive view of career development and counseling'. *Career Development and Counseling: Putting Theory and Research to Work,* edited by S.D. Brown and R.T. Lent. Hoboken, NJ: Wiley: 101–127.

Lent, R.W., Brown, S.D., and Hackett, G. 2002. 'Social cognitive career theory'. *Career Choice and Development* 4th ed., edited by D. Brown and Associate. San Francisco, CA: Jossey–Bass: 255–311.

Leung S.A. 2008. *The Big Five Career Theories, International Handbook of Career Guidance.* Springer, Dordrecht. https://doi.org/10.1007/978-1-4020-6230-8_6

Leung, S.A. 1995. 'Career counseling and development: A multicultural perspective'. *Handbook of Multicultural Counseling,* edited by J.G. Ponterotto, J.M. Casas, L.A. Suzuki, and C.M. Alexander. Thousand Oaks, CA: Sage :549–566.

Lips–Wiersma, M., and McMorland, J. 2006. 'Finding meaning and purpose in boundaryless careers: A framework for study and practice'. *Journal of Humanistic Psychology* 46: 147–167.

Lokan, J. 1984. *Manual of the Career Development Inventory,* Australian edition. Melbourne: Australian Council for Educational Research.

Maun, R. 2006. *My Boss is a Bastard: Surviving Turmoil at Work.* Marshall Cavendish.

McLeod, J. 1996. 'The emerging narrative approach to counselling and psychotherapy'. *British Journal of Guidance and Counselling* 24: 173–184.

McMahon, M. 2002. 'The Systems Theory Framework of career development: History and future prospects'. *Australian Journal of Career Development* 11 (3): 63–69.

McMahon, M., and Patton, W. 1995. 'Development of a systems theory of career development'. *Australian Journal of Career Development* 4: 15–20.

McMahon, M., and Patton, W. 2002. 'Using qualitative assessment in career counselling'. *International Journal of Educational and Vocational Guidance*: 51–66.

McMahon, M., and Patton, W. 2006. *Career Counselling: Constructivist Approaches*. London, UK: Routledge.

McMahon, M., Patton, W., and Tatham, P. 2003. *Managing Life, Learning and Work in The 21st Century: Issues Informing the Design of an Australian Blueprint for Career Development*. Subiaco, WA: Miles Morgan.

McMahon, M., Patton, W., and Watson, M. 2003. 'Developing qualitative career assessment processes'. *The Career Development Quarterly* 51: 194–202.

McMahon, M., Patton, W., and Watson, M. 2004. 'Creating career stories through reflection: An application of the Systems Theory Framework of career development'. *Australian Journal of Career Development* 13: 13–16.

McMahon, M., Patton, W., and Watson, M. 2005. *The My System of Career Influences MSCI and Facilitators Manual*. Camberwell, VIC: ACER Press.

McMahon, M., Watson, M., and Patton, W. 2005. 'Developing a qualitative career assessment process: The My System of Career Influences reflection activity'. *Journal of Career Assessment* 13: 476–490.

Mead, Elaine. 2020. 'Personal Strengths and Weaknesses Defined'. Positive Psychology. https://positivepsychology.com/what-are-your-strengths/.

Organization for Economic Cooperation and Development. 2004. Career guidance and public policy: bridging the gap. Paris: Author.

Patton, W. 1997.

Patton, W. and McMahon, M. 1999. *Career development and systems theory: A New Relationship*. Pacific Grove, CA: Brooks/Cole.

Patton, W. and McMahon, M. 2006. *Career Development and Systems Theory: Connecting Theory and Practice*. Rotterdam: Sense.

Patton, W. and McMahon, M. *Career Development in Practice: A Systems Theory Perspective*. Sydney, Australia: New Hobsons press: 1–13.

Peavy, R.V. 1992. 'A constructivist model of training for career counselors'. *Journal of Career Development* 18: 215– 229.

Peavy, R.V. 1998. *Sociodynamic Counselling: A Constructivist Perspective*. Victoria, Canada: Trafford.

Peavy, R.V. 2004. *Sociodynamic Counselling: A Practical Approach to Meaning Making*. Chagrin Falls, OH: Tao Institute.

Richardson, M.S. 1996. 'From career counseling to counseling/ psychotherapy and work, jobs, and career'. *Handbook of Career Counseling Theory and Practice*, edited by M.L. Savickas and W.B. Walsh. Palo Alto, CA: Davies–Black: 347–360.

Rounds, J., and Tracey, T.J. 1996. 'Cross–cultural structural equivalence of the RIASEC models and measures'. *Journal of Counseling Psychology* 43: 310–329.

Savickas, M.L. 1992. 'New directions in career assessment'. *Career Development: Theory and Practice*, edited by D.H. Montross and C.J. Shinkman. Springfield, IL: Charles C. Thomas: 336–355.

Savickas, M.L. 1993. 'Career counseling in the postmodern era'. *Journal of Cognitive Psychotherapy: An International Quarterly* 7: 205–215.

Savickas, M.L. 1997. 'Career adaptability: An integrative construct for life–span, life–space theory'. *Career Development Quarterly* 45: 247–259.

Savickas, M.L. 2000. 'Renovating the psychology of careers for the 21st century'. *The Future of Career*, edited by A. Collin and R.A. Young. Cambridge, UK: Cambridge University Press: 53–68.

Savickas, M.L. 2002. 'Career construction: A developmental theory of vocational behaviour'. *Career Choice and Development* 4th ed., edited by D. Brown and Associate. San Francisco, CA: Jossey–Bass: 149–205.

Savickas, M.L. 2005. 'The theory and practice of career construction'. *Career Development and Counseling: Putting Theory and Research to Work*, edited by S.D. Brown and R.T. Lent. Hoboken, NJ: Wiley: 42–70.

Savickas, M.L., and Lent, R.W. 1994. *Convergence in Career Development Theories: Implications for Science and Practice*. Palo Alto, CA: CPP Books.

Spokane, A.R., and Cruza–Guet, M.C. 2005. 'Holland's theory of vocational personalities in work environments'. *Career Development and Counseling: Putting Theory and Research to Work*, edited by S.D. Brown and R.T. Lent. Hoboken, NJ: Wiley: 24–41.

Spokane, A.R., Meir, E.I., and Catalano, M. 2000. 'Person–environment congruence and Holland's theory: A review and reconsideration'. *Journal of Vocational Behaviour* 57: 137–187.

Super, D.E. 1990. 'A life–span, life–space approach to career development'. *Career Choice and Development: Applying Contemporary Approaches to Practice* 2nd ed., edited by D. Brown and L. Brooks. San Francisco, CA: Jossey–Bass: 197–261.

Super, D.E., and Sverko, I. 1995. *Life Roles, Values and Careers: International Findings of Work Importance Study*. San Francisco, CA: Jossey–Bass.

Super, D.W. 1980. 'A life–span, life–space approach to career development'. *Journal of Vocational Behaviour* 16: 282–298.

Swanson, J.L., and Gore, P.A. 2000. 'Advances in vocational psychology theory and research'. *Handbook of Counseling Psychology* 3rd ed., edited by S.D. Brown and R.W. Lent. New York: Wiley: 233–269.

Tziner, A., Meir, E.I., and Segal, H. 2002. 'Occupational congruence and personal task–related attribute: How do they relate to work performance?' *Journal of Career Assessment* 10: 401–412.

Welch, J. and Byrne, J.A. 2003. *Jack: Straight from the Gut*. Grand Central Publishing.

Wendy Patton and Mary McMahon. 2014. *The Systems Theory Framework of Career Development and Counselling: Connecting Theory and Practice*, 3rd Edition. Brill

Zunker, V. G. 2002. *Career counseling: Applied concepts of life planning* 6th ed. Pacific Grove, CA: Brooks/Cole.

About Career Agility International

We are a team of career experts with decades of combined experience in Career Strategy consulting and career transition coaching.

Founded in 2017, Career Agility International has been helping our clients find Career Clarity and meaning in their lives. Our Career Partner programs involve a combination of workshops, online assessments, and personalized coaching sessions to help our clients unleash their full career potential and to build career resilience and satisfaction.

We also work with large corporate clients on employee engagement, corporate agility, employee resilience, and exit management programs. We are known for training HR and line managers on Career Agility coaching, enabling them to be more effective people leaders.

For retrenched employees, we provide them with highly personalized CareerCare Outplacement Support that ensure quick placement and more importantly, a robust Career Strategy that will help them enjoy increased employability and a more meaningful future.

'Besides being the world's first and only Career Strategy advisory firm, our biggest differentiator is that we care.'

Adrian Choo
CEO, Founder